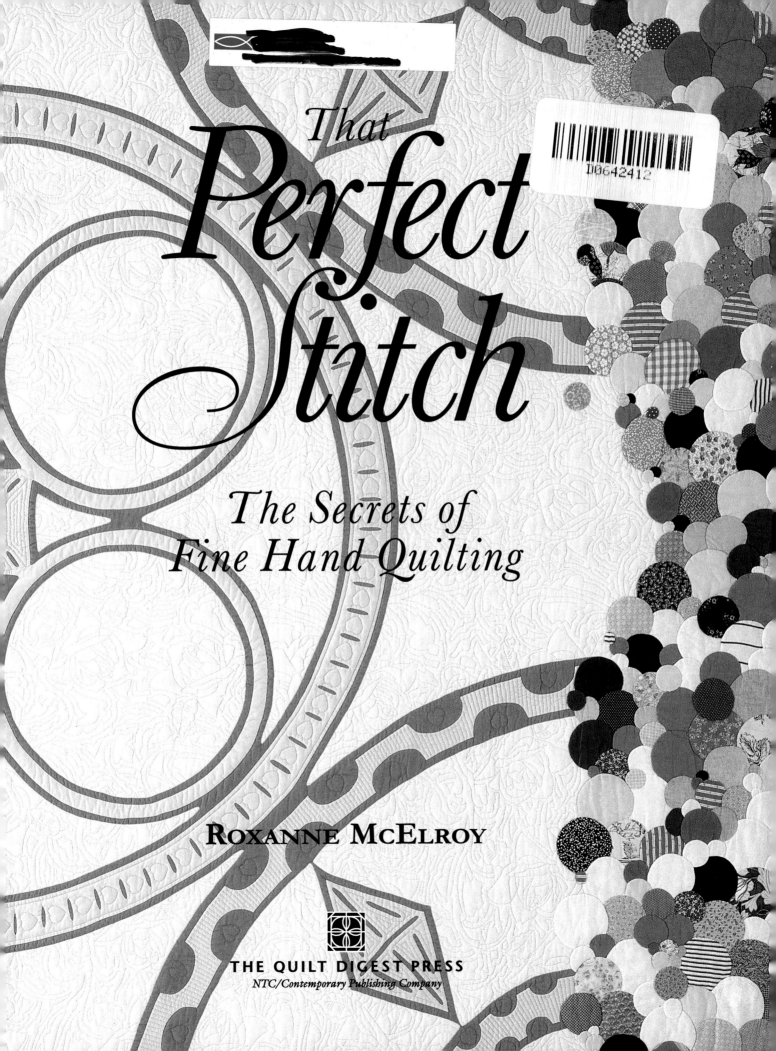

That Perfect Stitch

The Secrets of Fine Hand Quilting

ROXANNE McELROY

THE QUILT DIGEST PRESS

NTC/Contemporary Publishing Company

Library of Congress Cataloging-in-Publication Data

McElroy, Roxanne.
  That perfect stitch : the secrets of fine hand quilting / Roxanne McElroy.
    p.   cm.
  ISBN 0-8442-2652-1
    1. Quilting—Patterns.   2. Quilting—Equipment and supplies.   I. Title.
TT835.M3997   1997
746.46′042—dc21   97-15389
                                                                  CIP

Editorial direction by Anne Knudsen
Editorial production management by Gerilee Hundt
Art direction and book design by Kim Bartko
Cover design by Monica Baziuk
Cover photograph by Sharon Risedorph, San Francisco
Drawings by Kandy Petersen
Quilt photography by Sharon Risedorph, San Francisco
Photographs of quilts in settings and quilting tools by Sharon Hoogstraten, Chicago
Photographs of how-to steps by Sharon Risedorph, San Francisco
Manufacturing direction by Pat Martin

Published by The Quilt Digest Press
A division of NTC/Contemporary Publishing Group, Inc.
4255 West Touhy Avenue, Lincolnwood (Chicago), Illinois 60646-1975 U.S.A.
Copyright © 1998 by Roxanne McElroy
All rights reserved. No part of this book may be reproduced, stored in a retrieval
system, or transmitted in any form or by any means, electronic, mechanical,
photocopying, recording, or otherwise, without the prior permission of
NTC/Contemporary Publishing Group, Inc.
Printed in Hong Kong
International Standard Book Number: 0-8442-2652-1
    19 18 17 16 15 14 13 12 11 10 9 8 7 6 5 4 3 2

I would like to dedicate this book to my husband, Jeff.

Without him, my life and my art would be meaningless.

His logical mind tolerates my chaotic creative mind, and I only

hope that I have brought some levity and laughter into his life.

Together, we are a winning team!

Wedding Rings and Champagne Bubbles on a Bed of Roses.
Made by Roxanne McElroy.
The appliqué design is quite simple. It is the quilting design that makes this quilt special. Look for the petals and leaves within the design. Notice the thorns, too—a reminder that marriage is not always a bed of roses. A detail from the back of the quilt is shown on page xii.

CONTENTS

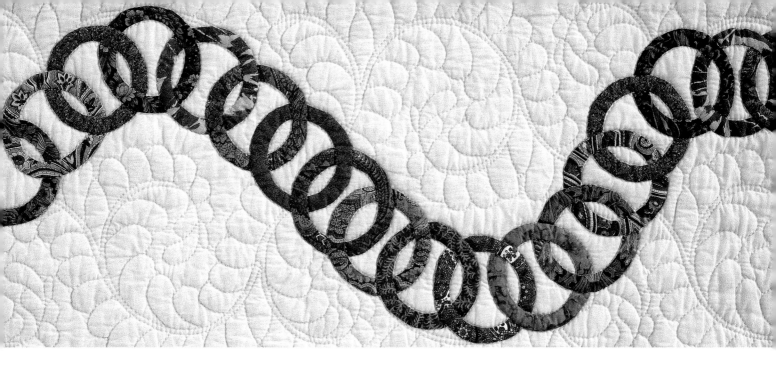

I would like to thank sincerely the quilters who so generously allowed their beautiful quilts to be photographed for my book. They are truly outstanding quilts with excellent workmanship. I would also like to thank my daughter, Didi, for practically forcing me into putting my class into written format. My thanks also to all my students who shared with me their successes and failures. I must also show my appreciation to P & B Textiles, Hoffman Fabrics, Colonial Needle Co., and Grace Frame Co. Without their specialized knowledge and willingness to answer my infinite number of questions, it would have been difficult indeed to come to the conclusions that I hope will help quilters everywhere achieve That Perfect Stitch.

A detail from the back of **Wedding Rings and Champagne Bubbles on a Bed of Roses,** *my mother's wedding gift to me.*

Dierdra McElroy

My mother, Roxanne McElroy, has always been larger than life. She never began a hobby with a simple project. Instead, she jumped in at the deep end, with projects that were challenging even for skilled artists. I sometimes think she could have been a scientist because the question "Why?" was always on her lips about everything she touched. She wanted to know why things worked or did not work, and never settled for simple answers. Her gregariousness and happiness were a contagion from which no one was immune. Hundreds of people have told me in confidence that Roxanne was the biggest motivator in their quilting and had a huge impact on their personal lives. She elicited people's self-confidence in such a positive way that careers were changed, marriages saved, and independence won.

Sadly, my mother passed away on April 13, 1997. We were at the first annual World Quilts & Textile show in Pasadena, California. She passed peacefully, although unexpectedly, in her sleep. The previous evening Roxanne had been honored to contribute to the first world panel of quilting teachers. The history, future, trends, and state of quilting in more than 10 nations was shared and discussed in a panel format. Roxanne felt this was a huge success, both politically and artistically.

Roxanne's never-ending quest for answers to her questions about quilting products made her a leading authority on the tools quilters use. She taught a class that was internationally known, in which she shared her research and her talents. Her unique ability to break difficult tasks down into separate manageable steps enabled all of her students to succeed. Many left her class quilting 14 stitches to the inch! I personally felt that her class had come into such demand that she could not possibly go everywhere to teach it. Writing a book would help her reach more quilters. Over the previous five years, several publishers had invited her to write a book, so I went and talked to them. When I found the company that could do her art justice, I took their representatives over to her and introduced them. Of course, I did not tell her that I had already told them she would do the book!

While she was writing, Roxanne complained that she spent more time at the computer than at her quilt frame. She complained that there were already hundreds of quilting books on the market (though very few were dedicated to hand quilting). But, she did it! Sadly, Roxanne left this world one week before getting to see the cover of her new book, *That Perfect Stitch*. I became more determined than ever that her work and ideas be published and made available to quilters. Fortunately, my mother taught me everything she knew, and I, too, have been teaching on the national circuit for a few years. I finished the last bit of the book as she would have wanted it, and I intend to continue her research and share her ideas and talents with the world.

My mother was my best friend, confidante, and business partner. She was truly the strongest woman I have ever known. She touched so many lives and always carried her own personal party with her everywhere she went. I love you, Mom!

Dierdra McElroy

My first experience with quilt making was in Tahiti, where I lived for several years. The first Christmas I was there, my housekeeper, Teiho, gave me a beautiful Tahitian quilt, called a Tifaifai, as a Christmas gift. Designed for tropical climates, Tifaifai are very similar to Hawaiian quilts, with one notable difference—Tifaifai are not quilted at all. They are made from lightweight fabric, intricately appliquéd, and simply hemmed around the edges to form a bedspread. I made six Tifaifai while I was in Tahiti. We used them on the beds and laundered them along with the sheets every week like clockwork. When I moved back to the United States, they were put in a closet and forgotten.

La Fusiere (The Fern). Made by Roxanne McElroy.
This is one of several Tifaifai I made in Tahiti, before I learned the quilting stitch. Once I learned to quilt, I transformed several of my Tifaifai into quilt tops.

Several years later, I was part of a group that hoped to raise funds by making a quilt to raffle. It did not matter that I had no idea how to quilt; I was one of a dozen women ready and willing to help out by learning this new craft. In less than an hour, it dawned on me that quilting was something I was very good at. One of the more experienced quilters in the group walked up behind me to check my stitches and said, "Oh no, dear. You must go through *all the layers*, not just the top." When I responded that I really believed I had done exactly that, she raised her eyebrows and dove for the floor under the quilt frame to prove me wrong. I will never forget it—six women on their hands and knees under the quilt frame looking in amazement at my work. In the next instant they were on their feet examining again the top of the quilt and asking me to demonstrate how I could achieve 14 stitches per inch (5.5 stitches per cm)! It was at that precise moment that I became a quilting instructor.

Very soon afterward I was making quilts of my own. My first project was to transform those wonderful Tifaifai I had appliquéd in Tahiti into quilts. Within months, I designed 10 Tifaifai patterns of my own and developed patterns for sale. I quilted one quilt for hire, wrote my first magazine article, taught my first class, and held my first lecture within a year of my first quilting stitches in 1987.

I inherited my quilting genes from my grandmother, Gladys Lee. But I was also lucky enough to inherit something just as important— the ability to break a task down into its individual components and so make it easier for someone else to learn. For a quilting teacher, that talent is even more valuable than a gift for quilting. I noticed very early on that sometimes my natural abilities alone were not enough to achieve a fine stitch, and I set about finding out why I could quilt 15 stitches per inch (6 stitches per cm) on one project but not nearly that many on another. My research led me down a very interesting path—a path down which I hope you will follow me as you turn the pages of this book.

All quilters are, or should be, concerned about the quality of their work. But quality is particularly important for hand quilters. The beauty of a handmade quilt is that, when done well, it endures to become an heirloom that is passed down through generations. Longevity, however, does not result from the skill of the quilter alone. Every product used in making the quilt—from the fabric and the batting to the needle, thread, and other supplies—contributes to the quality of the workmanship. Just as important, every technique the quilter uses affects the beauty and the life span of the quilt. The purpose of this book is to provide you with both the materials and the methods to help you achieve perfect stitches that last forever.

The book began as a reference for my class, That Perfect Stitch. I hope it will also become a source not only of techniques but also of inspiration for all of you who wish to improve your stitches and create more beautiful, longer-lasting quilts.

That Perfect Stitch

Fabric

When you look at antique quilts, you will see that almost all are made from cotton fabrics. There is a simple reason—in the early days of quilting, fabrics of any other fiber were extremely rare. Even today, when many other choices are available, those who make traditional quilts usually choose cotton in order to replicate the designs of the past. We have an enormous amount of freedom in the fabrics we choose, yet not all choices are conducive to achieving That Perfect Stitch. Some fabrics are simply more difficult to quilt than others, making tiny, even stitches impossible, no matter how expert the quilter. Once you understand the differences between fabrics and the ways in which they are made, you are better able to predict the effect on your stitch.

Balloons over New Mexico. Made by Roxanne McElroy.
A champagne glass design fills this quilt to the borders.

Mixing Fibers

If a quilter were to make two identical quilts, one of polyester-blend fabrics and one of 100 percent cotton, they would have an identical appraised value. The only thing that would reduce the value would be if the quilter mixed the two fibers within the same quilt. Polyester is stronger than cotton and so even a tiny patch of polyester in a cotton quilt will damage the quilt over time, or vice versa. For longevity, a balance of powers is needed.

Fabrics Suited to Quilting

It can take up to a thousand hours to make a quilt by hand. When we begin, we all have high hopes that the quilt we make will become a family heirloom and will pass down through generations. Yet no matter how beautiful the quilt or how carefully it is sewn, if it is not made from the right fabrics, it is not going to stand the test of time.

We know from seeing antique quilts that certain fabrics are more fragile than others and deteriorate more quickly. Silks, velvets, and satins, popular in antique crazy quilts, have rotted away in quilts that were frequently used or poorly cared for. Fabrics like these, because of their weave and texture, are impossible to hand quilt. Crazy quilts, after all, were tied rather than quilted. The same is true of flannel and wool fabrics. Although wool stands up to years of wear, the loose weave makes it unsuitable for hand quilting. The fibers in flannel are weak and, once the "fluff" of the individual yarns is worn away, the fabric is very sparse. Heavy fabrics like denim, corduroy, and double knits are equally inappropriate for hand quilting. Also, avoid any fabric that seems to stretch when pulled on the straight of the grain. These fabrics are too unstable; the quilting process draws the fabric in the direction you are quilting, and you will most likely have a rippled quilt when you are finished.

The Weave of the Fabric

The fabrics we choose have to meet other requirements, besides the ability to stand the test of time. First, the weave must be right. The ideal fabric for hand quilting is one that is woven at about 75 threads per inch (30 threads per cm) in each direction. If the weave is too tight, it makes quilting an almost impossible task. Pima cotton is woven 132 yarns per inch (52 yarns per cm) to the weft and 100 yarns per inch (40 yarns per cm) to the warp! Bedsheets are generally made from pima cotton and that is the main reason why you should never use a bedsheet to back a quilt.

The weave of some fabrics is too loose to quilt well, especially if your stitches are small. The smaller your stitches become, there will be a time when you see that they are so small that the needle can actually rise and descend through the fabric without catching a single yarn of the quilt top or backing. This means you are simply too good for that particular fabric! Any fabric that is woven less than 60 yarns per inch

(24 yarns per cm) to the warp and 60 yarns per inch (24 yarns per cm) to the weft will produce this effect for better quilters.

To compound this problem, fabrics with a loose weave are usually heavier than others, meaning that each yarn is fatter in diameter. After having carefully observed several hundred quilting stitches under a microscope, I have determined that quilting will never split the yarn of a fabric. In every single case, the yarn rolls in one direction or the other and forces the point of the needle through the intersections between yarns. This means that if the yarn is too fat, the needle simply will not go where you want it to, resulting in uneven stitches.

Crossover Fabrics

Crossover fabrics—those that are originally designed for clothing or decorating, not specifically for quilting—are usually too loosely woven and often too unevenly woven to quilt. Yet, because the color and prints are appealing, we sometimes find it hard to resist them. Manufacturers rarely specialize in quilting fabrics, so crossover fabrics can be found in most name brands. This is a good reason to stick to your quilt shop when hunting for fabrics. Unfortunately, the number of yarns per inch (cm) is not listed on the end of fabric bolts. Indeed, I often wonder if the manufacturers themselves fully comprehend the effect a yarn count can have on the hand-quilting stitch. It is up to you to train your eye to look past the gorgeous prints and colors to the actual fabric construction and decide whether the weave is too loose or too tight for quilting. You can also arm yourself with a magnifying lens and ruler when going to the quilt shop!

Grades of Fabric

Not only do manufacturers make different fabrics for different purposes, they also create more than one grade of each fabric type. Second-grade fabrics are less expensive, and for very good reasons. Some are not only low in thread count, but the individual yarns from which they are made are thinner, making the weave very loose and resulting in a lightweight fabric. On top of that, the thread count is often inconsistent across the fabric. Some leading manufacturers print identical designs on first- and second-grade fabrics, marketing one to quality quilt shops and the other under a different name to chain stores

Warp and Weft

Yarns are threads woven to make fabrics. Yarns that run parallel to the selvages are the warp of the fabric; yarns that run across from selvage to selvage are the weft. It is easy—just remember "weft is left!"

Mermaids in the Surf. Made by Roxanne McElroy.

Echo-quilted with simple outline quilting around appliqué of waves. Can you tell which of the background fabrics was not prewashed?

and discount stores. Therefore, if you see a discounted fabric carrying a name brand, look at it very carefully before you buy. To be sure, pull out the trusty magnifier and ruler to check the thread count!

You can sometimes find wonderful fabrics at discount prices—all that is wrong with them is that the colors did not print quite right. Some fabrics have as many as 17 colors and each one must be stamped separately onto the fabric. If even one of those colors is slightly out of place or is missing altogether the fabric is discarded by the manufacturer and sold only as a second-grade fabric to discount stores, if sold at all. The consumer will not be able to tell there is a color problem. As a general rule of thumb, before you buy any discounted fabric, first check the thread count. If it looks good and you like the design, buy it.

The Mathematics of It All

A quilter intentionally sets out to quilt 10 stitches per inch (4 stitches per cm). Her fabric is a 60/60 (24/24) thread count. Divide 60 by 10 to make 6 (divide 24 by 4 to make 6). She must use 6 threads to complete each individual stitch, which means 3 threads must pass over the needle and 3 threads must pass under the needle. You can see that trying to quilt any more than 10 stitches per inch (4 stitches per cm) on this fabric would be impossible. The quilter would be weaving, not stitching! Likewise once you understand the mathematics it becomes plain that fabrics with uneven thread counts can cause uneven quilting stitches. A quilter may be quilting 14 stitches per inch (5.5 stitches per cm) traveling to the weft on a 78/56 (30/22) thread count fabric, but as soon as she changes directions (which is inevitable) she is relegated to less than 10 per inch (4 stitches per cm), no matter how hard she may try.

Quality Quilting Fabrics

In terms of thread count, balance (equal thread count to the warp and the weft), and quality of dyes, some of the finest cotton quilting fabrics are manufactured by Hoffman, RJR, P & B, Alexander Henry, and South Seas Imports. I have always found Lunn Fabrics to be the most creative and best quality hand-dyed fabrics around. In several fabrics from Concord and Peter Pan, and even in some from VIP, the weaves are not balanced—there can be as many as 20 more yarns per inch (8 yarns per cm) to the warp than there are to the weft.

Desert Storm. Made by Bonnie Kosler-Kubacki, The Woodlands, TX.
This wonderful quilt features crosshatching, stitch-in-the-ditch, and quilting over folded fabric.
The stitches are just as exquisite on the reverse of the quilt as they are on the front.

Quilting Painted Fabrics

Painted fabrics are more difficult to quilt than other fabrics because the paint is a foreign substance that has to be penetrated by the needle before it can get through the fiber itself. The heavier the paint, the harder the quilt job. Paint on fabric has, in the past, yellowed with age. Heavily painted fabrics can even crack and peel. Remember, paint is a surface application only. Lightly painted fabrics can be washed off in several washings or wear off with time. Beautiful gold and silver accent prints are no exception. I am personally drawn to these fabrics for their stunning beauty. I use them and love them, knowing full well the paint will be gone by the time my grandchild inherits. Remember, one secret to enjoying quilting is not compromising your choices to a point that it makes quilting a chore—enjoy painted fabrics while they last!

Should Quilters Prewash Fabrics?

I prewash all my fabrics, but I have come across many quilters who are reluctant to do so. Some prefer not to prewash because they like the feel of the fiber with the original sizing still in it. (Sizing is the process through which manufacturers press a finishing coat onto a fabric to give it extra body.) There is a simple remedy for this, however—using spray sizing or even spray starch when the fabric is pressed will replenish the original look and feel. Other quilters think that the fabric somehow changes in the washing process. In fact, there are only a very few fabrics that "change." Examples include chintz, sateen, and polished cottons. Since the unique sheen on these fabrics is a surface treatment done through a heat-pressing process, the sheen naturally goes away with washing. These fabrics are exciting and add an interesting look to a new quilt. I have made quilts using them, knowing full well that the sheen would disappear. Sometimes, I just cannot resist these fabrics and feel that, however temporary, that lovely effect is worth the effort while it lasts.

There are a couple of overwhelming arguments in favor of prewashing your fabrics. First, fabric tends to shrink. In the manufacturing process, fabrics are woven to a standard 48″ (120 cm) wide, selvage to selvage. During the dyeing and printing process a print cloth will usually shrink by about 3″ (8 cm). When the fabric reaches your quilt shop it is usually about 44″ to 45″ (110 cm to 115 cm) wide, as indicated on the ends of the bolts. Crossover fabrics shrink a little more due to their weight and the thickness of the yarn, coming into the shops at about 43″ (109 cm) wide. The yarns found in homespun fabrics are of a nature that they shrink drastically, sometimes to less than 41″ (104 cm) wide! Simple logic tells us that a quilt made with dozens or even hundreds of different fabrics that were not prewashed will become severely puckered with its first washing. In time, the fabrics that do not shrink much will put excess stress on the ones that shrink drastically, tearing them out of the quilt.

The second argument for always prewashing your fabrics revolves around the dyes that are used. No matter what a manufacturer says, fabric dyes are still unstable. Some are worse than others, obviously, but there is no way to tell by just looking at a fabric which ones will cause trouble. Prewashing fabrics in solutions of salt or vinegar can sometimes help set the colors. There is also a product on the market called Retayne that has had good reviews. Never trust that fabrics will be colorfast—there are few things in quilting more devastating than seeing colors bleed into surrounding fabrics.

I wash all my fabrics in a regular machine-wash cycle and dry them on a regular setting, too. I am not gentle and do not believe in using the gentle cycle for quilting fabrics. I check the water in the final rinse by removing some of it in a clear glass cup. If the water has any tint at all, the fabric gets washed again. I do this three times and then, if the fabric is still throwing off dyes, I do not use it in my quilt and neither should you. It is as simple as that.

There are quilters out their that say their quilts will simply never be washed. It is true, you could put a label on the back of your quilt saying "over my dead body wash this quilt!" That is exactly what will happen. One of your family members will feel compelled to wash the quilt no matter what your wishes might have been. It happens all the time!

Ironing Fabric

It has been my observation that quilters tend to iron their fabrics far too much. While most quilters worry about washing fabrics, they do not seem to realize the damage is done by excessive ironing. Irons can heat to more than 360°F (182°C), which is hot enough to scorch cotton. This is akin to the techniques used to obtain polished cottons. Iron your fabric only as much as needed to take out creases. Avoid coming to a rest with the iron in any one particular spot. Pressing the iron down in one place allows a build-up of extreme heat that has no escape and severely damages the yarns of the fabric. A good example would be to look at a pair of jeans that you iron regularly. Look at where you usually iron in the creases, and you will notice that the color is faded. This is a sign of damaged fibers caused from extreme heat build-up on the fold.

Quilter's Workshop

1. Piece together 20 5″ × 5″ (12 cm × 12 cm) squares of different fabric brands. Mark the brand name on each square with a permanent pen. Using a good polyester batting and a muslin backing, sandwich and baste the practice quilt together. With a waxed quilting thread in a color that is easily visible and your favorite brand of needle in a size 10, quilt a simple design on each block. On the back of your sampler mark your impressions on the ease of quilting. You might even want to get a magnifying lens and take note of the thread count.

2. Pull a couple of ½ yard (0.5 m) pieces of red fabric from your stash and wash them along with a piece of pure white cotton fabric. At the last rinse cycle, stop the machine and dip a clear cup into the tub for a sample of water. Evaluate for clarity. When the cycle is complete, remove the fabrics and inspect them. Did the white fabric absorb any red dye? Repeat this experiment with different red fabrics, making note of brand names, if possible.

CHAPTER TWO

Batting

From old blankets to horsehair, all kinds of materials have been used to stuff quilts. Some of our ancestors were lucky and could use cotton, picked from nearby fields. Other quilters, however, were desperate enough to use horsehair or even dog hair. One recently discovered antique quilt was batted with newspaper! A rather unusual quilt in Hawaii even had tobacco leaves for batting. We are fortunate today to have a multitude of batting choices, each with a different feel and look. We can choose from cotton, polyester, cotton-polyester blend, wool, and silk. Some battings are easier to quilt than others, and each gives a quilt a different finished look and feel. There is no right or wrong choice to be made in battings; it is simply a matter of deciding which look and feel you want.

Tiare de Tahiti. Made by Roxanne McElroy.
The national flower of Tahiti is quilted in 1/2 inch (2.25 cm) echo.

Kang Kang Sul Le.
Made by Yong Ho Halt.
With wide stippling on the mountain and bushes, the quilting design follows the fabric pattern itself. The quilter used fabric paints for highlights and shadows for the pagoda.

Batting Fibers

Cotton

The time-honored batting is, of course, cotton. Cotton is a natural fiber and generally produces a soft and cuddly quilt. Cotton is a good choice, because it is time proven and it does not *beard*—a phenomenon where batting fibers poke up through fabrics in a finished quilt. Other battings simply have not been around long enough to know how they will wear over time. I suspect that all batts flatten or break up into clumps, given enough time.

If it is important to you to use a natural fiber in your batting you are limited to cotton, wool, or silk. One appeal of cotton is that it is cooler to sleep under than the other two choices. It is also less expensive and more easily found. A problem with cotton batts is that they do not needle as well as polyester, and so the quilting stitches are not quite perfect. For this reason, if I use a cotton batting, I have to consider it as one compromise in my quilt. You can expect shrinkage of 3 percent from most brands of cotton batting. Some are designed to shrink a little more for that "antique puckered" look, which is nice if that is what you want.

Another problem with cotton is that some brands have not rid their product of cotton seed sloughs. Quilting into these can cause finger joint pain as well as uneven quilting stitches as the quilter is forced to go around the seed. It is not unheard of for the oils that these seeds contain to migrate out into the quilt top, staining it permanently.

Some quilters like to limit the amount of quilting and spread their stitching more than 2″ (5 cm) apart. If you are using cotton batting, you need to quilt more densely than this. I personally quilt every 1″ (2.5 cm) to ensure that the layers meld into a single unit.

Polyester

Polyester battings come in several thicknesses and each has a different use and look. Mixing a polyester batting into a cotton quilt will not,

according to quilt appraisers, devalue your quilt in any way. What the polyester does for you is provide a much more "slippery pathway" than cotton for your needle to glide through. I always look for a polyester batting that appears to have an even thickness throughout. This is easy to see when you hold the batting up to a light.

Wool

Wool battings have been used for generations and are especially popular in colder climates. Wool batting is the warmest batt you can use. Most wool battings launder as well as polyester batts, and I have always found them to be very smooth and easy to quilt. The major flaw with woolen batts, however, is that they tend to beard, the batting fibers working their way up through the quilt top. Bearding can

Batting Brands

Brand	Fiber	Features	Effect on Stitch
Hobb's Washable Wool	Wool	Take care to use quality quilting fabrics and to quilt closely to avoid bearding, which is more common with wool batts. A little more expensive than other batts, this brand does not require special care in laundering. It makes for a warm quilt to sleep under.	Produces fine quilting stitches
Warm & Natural Wool	Wool	As above	Needles well and produces nice stitches
Mountain Mist Blue Ribbon	Cotton	This batting is designed to be quilted then washed. It will fall apart in the washer if you try to prewash it. It shrinks by about 3 to 5 percent, making it ideal for creating an antique puckered look.	Needles easily, producing beautiful quilts
Hobb's Heirloom	Cotton	As above	As above
Hobb's Organic	Cotton	For hand quilting, make sure you get the batting *without scrim*—a fine netting attached to one side to act as a stabilizer for machine quilting.	Satisfactory
Warm & Natural	Cotton	This batting is coarse and stiff and has many slubs that get in the way of the needle. Prewashing does not help. Seed oils from the slubs can stain the quilt after it is finished.	Causes stitches to look uneven, as quilter dodges slubs. Unsuitable for hand quilting
Quilter's Dream Cotton	Cotton	This company offers several lofts of batting. Their "Request" style batting is soft, natural colored, and even in thickness. No pre-washing is necessary, resulting in a minimal 1% to 2% shrinkage in a finished quilt.	Produces even stitches without excess strain. This is one of my favorite battings.
Fairfield Soft Touch	Cotton	A pristine white batting that is very smooth and evenly pressed. No prewashing is necessary.	This is my favorite cotton batting, giving me smaller stitches than any other.
Fairfield Cotton Classic	80% Cotton 20% Polyester	As the factory sprays a thin silicon coating on the batting to make it easier to package, it requires special treatment before use. This coating will not hurt a quilt, it only makes it harder to needle. Unroll and soak the batt in cool water for a few minutes. Hand wring and put in the dryer on a polyester setting. It may take a couple of cycles to dry. Once treated, this batting makes a soft, cuddly quilt any child—or adult—would love.	Needles well, once washed

Brand	Fiber	Features	Effect on Stitch
Hobb's Fat Batt	Polyester	Designed for tied, comforter style quilts. The loft is too high to hand quilt well.	Produces large, uneven stitches. Unsuitable for hand quilting
Fairfield Hi Loft	Polyester	As above	As above
Fairfield Extra Loft	Polyester	A unique batting that squishes down to make very fine quilting stitches and then puffs up in between stitched lines to give the quilt a comforter look.	Quilts nicely. Avoid quilting too closely, or the special features of the high loft are defeated.
Mountain Mist Quilt Light	Polyester	This is a medium to low loft batt that is very even. It consistently unrolls out of the bag easily without folds or kinks.	My favorite polyester batt, it allows for tiny, even stitches.
Hobb's Thermore	Polyester	Originally made for wearable arts, this batt has virtually no loft. It is very evenly woven and makes lightweight quilts.	Produces small, even stitches, but little relief
Fairfield Low Loft	Polyester	This batting is even thinner than Hobb's Thermore, but it does have some loft. Sometimes we compromise a quilt with an extra heavy fabric. Using an extra-thin batting can often reverse the compromise.	Though it needles well, this batting seems too thin for quilting, as a finished quilt can feel like it lacks any stuffing at all.
Fairfield Traditional	Polyester	A good choice for a quilt that is heavy but not thick. It is reminiscent of years gone by when quilters used old flannel blankets as batting.	Produces a heavy quilt with fine stitches
Hobb's Poly-Down	Polyester	A medium loft batting, that tends to be uneven, with high and low areas	Causes uneven stitches as the quilter passes through denser and thinner areas
Hobb's Black Batt	Polyester	A black version of Hobb's Poly-Down, designed for Amish quilts that tend to be darker in overall color. The black batt makes fibers that migrate to the surface less visible. Be sure to test lighter fabrics against the batt before using it.	As above

Based on my personal examinations of products I have used

Black Batt

Not all batting is white. Battings range from pure snowy white to ecru to black! Hobb's Black Batt was designed to use in Amish quilts where the majority of the fabrics are dark. The idea was to limit the effects of bearding by making escaped fibers less noticeable. Using black batting also helps maintain the integrity of the colors, since sometimes white behind blacks and dark blues makes them look a little faded or washed out. If you are making an Amish quilt and plan to use black batt, it might be a good idea to take your quilt top into the store and lay the lightest fabric in it over the package of black batt. Occasionally the batt will shadow through lighter colors, defeating the purpose of the batt. Doing this ahead of time could avoid disappointments.

be heart-wrenching—the quilt looks as though a Persian cat took a nap on it, but whenever you pull the hairs off they are replaced by more! No one knows for sure what causes bearding, but my research has shown that eight out of ten times a wool batting was used, often in conjunction with a loose weave fabric. The spacing of the quilting may also have something to do with it, since I have never seen a heavily quilted quilt—with quilting lines no more than 1" (2.5 cm) apart— beard.

Silk

The most exotic batting I have found is 100 percent silk. It must be unrolled carefully onto the quilt back and smoothed and fussed with a little more than other battings. Silk batting has a "clingy" quality that is a real advantage because it does not shift around between the layers of the quilt while you stitch. To quote one fellow quilter, "It quilts just like a hot knife through butter." It produces fine, even stitches with great ease on the hand. The silk batting I use is made from mulberry trees grown in China, and it launders the same as polyester. A quilt made with silk batting is warmer than a cotton or polyester quilt but not as warm as a wool quilt. The only disadvantage to silk batting, besides the extra effort in laying it out, is the cost. Still, silk batting will give you the most sensual quilt you'll ever make!

Batting Loft

The *loft* of a quilt describes the degree to which the quilt puffs up around the quilting stitches. The loft of the batting you choose is really a matter of personal taste. In years past, high-loft battings have been popular, while more recently the trend has been toward a thinner look. There are no rules regarding which batting is appropriate for a specific type of quilt. You may want to consider the ease of quilting—higher loft battings are a little harder to quilt. Take into consideration, too, the purpose of the quilt. If it is a wall hanging, a lower loft lies flatter against the wall and creates smaller dust-collecting ledges!

Preparing Batting for Quilting

Whichever batting you select, it is always a good idea to open the package and unroll the batting. Allow it to lie flat on a bed, table, or floor for 24 hours before sandwiching it in a quilt. This allows the crinkles to settle and smooth out. The batting should be about 4" (10 cm) wider and 4" (10 cm) longer than the quilt top. It can be cut to fit later. If the batting is too small, two pieces can be joined by butting them up together and sewing with large overcast stitches. Do not allow overlapping.

Quilter's Workshop

Select as many batts as possible and cut them into small squares. Join them together by using overcast stitches. Sandwich the pieced batting with muslin and mark each batting name on the quilt backing. Using simple templates, trace a design on the muslin over each different batting. Quilt each with the same size and type of needle and the same brand of thread. Compare the results and write them in permanent ink in each square on the back of the quilt.

CHAPTER THREE

Needles

Most of us take needles for granted. All we consider when we choose one from a new pack is the size of the eye, and, after that, we barely think twice about it. The only time we get out a new needle is if we lose or break the first one. Considering that needles are the key tool in hand quilting, we really should think carefully about the choices we make and the ways in which we use them. For it is only when you use the needle that is perfect for the quilt you are making that you will be able to achieve That Perfect Stitch. All needles wear and dull with use, and that use should not exceed 8 to 10 hours per needle. Look for the best-quality needle at a price at which you will feel no guilt about throwing it away for a fresh one.

Jewell's Paradise. Made by Roxanne McElroy.
The circles radiating out from the center draw the eye to the border of the quilt which is echo-quilted, with hibiscus blossoms in relief.

How the Very Best Needles Are Made

Needle making started as a cottage industry in the late 1700s. There are only five needle factories in the world, in the Czech Republic, India, England, Japan, and China. The very best needles are made in the British factories, where labor positions are so highly valued that jobs are often handed down from parent to child in the laborer's will! The factories have never become fully automated, so needles have been made in almost the same way for hundreds of years. Skills passed down through the ages have resulted in a quality and pride of workmanship that is unmatched.

Wire

Wire drawn and cut to two needle lengths

Wire pointed at both ends.

Wire stamped with impression of two eyes

The eyes punched through

Wire broken into two needles

Cheeked—waste metal ground off sides of the eye

Headed—top of the eye rounded

Hardened

Tempered

Scoured

Nickel plated

Needle Test

I examined many of the top brands of quilting needles—all size 10 Betweens. I checked the shaft for thickness and strength; the plating for thickness or the presence of burrs; the point for the proper taper; and the eye for comparative size. I also considered value for money. On a scale of 1 to 10 (1 is poor, 10 is excellent), I assigned a rating to each brand. Here are my results.

Richard Hemming	10	St. Thomas & Sons	9
Roxanne's Needles	10	Clover	8.5
John James	9.75	Piecemakers	5
Boye	9.75	All platinum & gold	3
Colonial	9	EZ International	1
J.P. Coats	9		

All ratings are based on my personal examinations of products I have used

The top needle is an example of a poorly shaped needle. The tip will penetrate fabric easily, then stall at the ridge, causing the quilter unconsciously to push a little harder. Then the ridge will suddenly clear by slipping, causing a momentary lack of control and perhaps the difference between 10 stitches per inch (4 stitches per cm) and 14 stitches per inch (5.5 stitches per cm). A good needle should taper gradually from the eye directly to a point as portrayed below.

How Needles Are Made

All quilting needles, known as Betweens, are made from five-gauge wire that arrives at the factory on spools as big as automobile tires. First, the wire is stretched, which causes it to become thinner. When the wire reaches the specific requirements for the size needle to be made, it is cut into sections the length of two needles. Both ends of each section are ground to a point. Then the center of each section is pressed flat with two dimpled spots. Holes are punched through each of these dimples and the eyes are formed. A laborer then snaps the needle sections in half, separating the two needles. Through a process called "cheeking," waste metal is ground off the sides of the eyes and the top is rounded. The needle as it stands is too weak to be used so it is tempered to harden the metal. It is then prepared for plating by being scoured. Plating is essential as it strengthens the needle and provides a slippery surface so that it can glide easily through fabric. Most needles are plated with nickel, although some use gold or even platinum. The needles are then weighed and counted, wrapped in packages, and proudly stamped, "Made in England."

Choosing a Needle

Betweens quilting needles range from the largest, size 1, to the smallest, size 12. The most commonly used sizes are 8 through 12, although, curiously, there is no size 11. The larger the number the smaller the needle. In a good brand of needle the diameter of the shaft will proportionately get smaller or larger as the length changes. Therefore, size 12 needles are not only smaller in length but in diameter as well. It is generally agreed the smaller the needle, the easier it goes through the fabric and batting layers of a quilt. Yet there comes a point where the smallness of the needle compromises its strength—a benefit in one area creates a handicap in another. The trick is to find the best needle for you, based upon the way in which you sew. For example, I have strong fingers and my stitching is forceful. I cannot use size 12 quilting needles because I snap them in two when I try to stack my first bunch of stitches! Size 10, or even sometimes size 9, works best for me.

Needle wire on its own is weak. The more it is stretched to make a smaller needle the weaker it becomes. Five-gauge wire has a uniform size, but different factories stretch it to different degrees, and this is a determining factor in needle quality. If the wire is stretched too much, the needle is so thin that it can be snapped in two with little effort. A

Sharp Points

Though it is possible to buy gadgets that claim to sharpen dull points, such as special pin cushions filled with grain sand, do not be fooled into using them. The only way to sharpen is to grind to a better point, right? Doing that would mean grinding away the plating, exposing the rough, porous needle wire which will cause even more drag than a dull point. Needles are cheap—simply throw them away when the points dull and start with a fresh one.

Shamrock Fantasy. Made by Hazel Canny.
This sensational white-on-white, king-size quilt demonstrates tiny stitches in stippling and trapunto.

bent or broken needle is useless to quilters. Under pressure, better quality needles will bend instead of snap.

Plating

All needles must be plated for strength and smoothness, since the raw wires are too coarse to pass through fabrics without catching. While only very obvious flaws are visible to the naked eye, a magnifying glass will show them clearly. The thickness of the plating is impossible to see, however. If the plating, no matter how even, is too thin, the life span of the needle is shortened considerably. A needle with good nickel plating will last for several hours of quilting before the finish starts to wear thin. You can usually tell when the plating begins to wear because of the added drag on the needle as it is pulled through the layers of a quilt. This is a signal that it is time to throw the needle away and start with a fresh one.

Nickel is the most commonly used plating material, but sometimes gold or platinum is used. The finish on those needles is not any smoother than nickel-plated needles. Both are more expensive than nickel—a single platinum needle, for example, can cost as much as an entire pack of nickel-plated needles. In fact, there is only one benefit I can think of to justify the additional expense of these needles—some people have an allergy to nickel that prevents them from quilting. It can cause a severe rash. Gold or platinum needles sometimes can provide relief.

Plating can be eroded by the acidity of a quilter's perspiration. If you notice that your fingers tend to perspire when quilting, you need only change your needles more frequently than other quilters.

Point

A quality needle has a point that tapers very gradually from just below the eye all the way down to the point, so that it moves effortlessly through the layers of a quilt. Some factories take short cuts when making needles. For example, in order to make a size 12 Betweens, they take a size 10, shorten it to the required length, and stick a new point on it (see page 20). This leaves a slight ridge above the point where the point-to-shaft transition occurs. It takes extra force to move that ridge through the layers of a quilt, which means the quilter pushes a little harder.

Needle Size

Though some say the smaller the needles, the more skilled the quilter, this is simply not true! After all, a machine sewer would choose a big, strong needle when machine-sewing denim and a small, delicate needle when machine-sewing silk. The same principle holds for hand quilters. With heavy fabric and several seam allowances, only a large needle can penetrate the layers, turn, and resurface without bending or snapping. The key is to use the smallest needle possible to get the job done—that, after all, is why needles are available in such a variety of sizes.

Jungle Glow. Made by Roxanne McElroy.

The appliqué design in this quilt is very complicated, so simple outline quilting was sufficient to set it off.

Once the ridge has been passed, the needle tends to slip suddenly causing stitches twice as big as they should be.

The point is the most delicate part of the needle. It is easily damaged when dropped or poorly stored. Often, needles that are carried in metal or flat plastic cases can end up with bent or "jammed" points when they slam against the sides of the case. Barely visible to the naked eye, jammed points are very easy to see through a strong magnifying glass. You can feel them when you are quilting, too. The needle feels blunt as you push it through the layers and tends to catch on quilt fibers when you pull it out.

Eye

Never believe that the smaller the eye, the better the needle. After all, any time a needle's eye is smaller in diameter than the quilting thread we use, then that needle becomes useless to us. Consider it defective! Some very small needles have large eyes, and those are the ones we should choose. Even large-eye needles, made to help those of us whose eyesight is less than perfect, can pass quality tests with flying colors.

Improvements in needles will be slight in coming years. It might be interesting to see if the plating might be colored for better visibility in fabrics. If the industry offered packages of needles in several colors, then the quilter could choose the most highly visible one for a specific quilting job. They would be more visible when lost in the carpet as well!

Quilter's Workshop

1. Take out all the different brands of needles you have in your sewing basket or buy a selection of brands. Make sure they are all the same size needle. Through a microscope or under a magnifying lens, examine each one for strength, plating, eye, and point construction. Take thorough notes on each brand and then assign a quality rating to each one.
2. Prepare a small "quilt sandwich" of backing, low-loft batting, and a muslin quilt top. Using the needles you rated in the previous exercise, quilt a few stitches with each, noting the differences. Which needle gave you the best stitches with the least effort? Repeat with different needle sizes to determine the size that might be best for you and this particular project.

CHAPTER FOUR

Thread

Ideally, early quilters liked to use a coarse cotton thread, generally referred to as "20 count." It was known for its strength and endurance. In reality, however, they used whatever thread they could get hold of, availability being the key factor. Much of the time, regular sewing thread was all they could get at the general store. To strengthen it, they would run the thread through beeswax before quilting with it. Though some quilters still use beeswax, we are fortunate not only to have guidance on which threads will provide the best work, but to have easy access to those products as well. Modern threads come in a multitude of colors and fibers and are available waxed or unwaxed. You can now choose threads to match the purpose of your quilt.

Tricycles and Trains. Made by Roxanne McElroy.
First I echo-quilted four times around the outline, leaving bare spots that I did not quite know how to fill. So I flipped the quilt over and appliquéd teddy bears on the back and echo-quilted those four times, too.

Old El Paso. Made by Roxanne McElroy.

Some quilts dictate the quilting design.

Collection of Adele Mozek, The Woodlands, TX

Not All Thread Is the Same

There is an enormous difference between sewing and quilting thread. Quilting thread must be strong in order to withstand the stress put on it by quilting. Sewing thread is 30 to 50 percent weaker than quilting thread and is simply not strong enough for quilting. We now know that beeswax, painstakingly applied to thread by our ancestors, does not strengthen sewing thread. If regular sewing thread is used, you must quilt as close as every ½″ (1 cm) so that the strain on each line of quilting is reduced. Even so, I cannot recommend regular sewing thread for quilting.

There is also a great difference between thread manufactured for hand quilting and thread manufactured for machine quilting. Contrary to popular belief, the two are not interchangeable. Think for a moment of how the sewing machine operates. Any given spot on the thread has to be strong enough to be forced down through the quilt top, batting, and backing *just once*. It also has to be soft in texture so it will go through the mechanisms of the machine, without causing excess fuzz. The thread used for hand quilting has to be made differently to be strong enough. An 18″ (45 cm) length of thread is pulled through all the layers of a quilt not once but up to 100 times, with tremendous wear on the entire length of the thread. A good hand-quilting thread is made without a knap and is heavily waxed to prevent excessive knotting or tangling.

Knap

Thread is made of very short lengths of cotton staple, twisted together and wrapped onto a spool. The ends of these short staples stick out of the thread, making it appear "hairy" when viewed under a microscope. The hairs tend to stick out in the exact same direction. This is the thread's *knap*. When the thread is waxed, the knap sticks to the twisted surface. The result is a smoother thread that is easier to pull through

fabric and that tends not to tangle.

Because of the knap, the direction in which you pull thread through the fabric is important. If you pull against the knap, you make the staples of the thread stick out even farther, giving your

Waxing Thread

It certainly is possible for you to take the trouble to pull each strand of your regular unwaxed quilting thread through a chunk of beeswax, just as our ancestors did. But this coats only the *outside* of the thread and most of the wax is wiped off the first time the thread is pulled through fabric. To get the wax to penetrate the fibers of the thread, you could run an iron over the waxed thread. Even so, it is impossible to get even coverage along the strand. Since factory-waxed threads are readily available and are superior to hand-waxed threads, why would you want to waste your precious quilting time standing at the ironing board?

Ironing

If you do not match the thread to the fabric, ironing can severely damage the threads in your quilt. Cotton scorches at 360°F (182°C) and polyester melts at 385°F (196°C). Polyester heats up at a rate almost twice as fast as cotton. Quilters who are obsessed with ironing can damage the thread in their quilts by constant ironing, especially if the thread is polyester. The damage is worse with patchwork than appliqué. When both seam allowances are pressed to one side, the running stitch is exposed directly to the iron. Remember, polyester heats twice as fast and does not give a scorch warning before meltdown.

thread a fuzzy quality. As a comparison, just think of what would happen if you were to stick a feather through a buttonhole backward. The feather would become ruffled. By pulling against the grain of the knap—referred to in the industry as "runback of twist"—you are roughing up the thread. This makes it more difficult to pull smoothly through the fabric and results in many more tangles and knots.

In most cases, the process of wrapping thread onto a spool flattens and smoothes the knap in one direction. If you always knot the end of the thread that comes off the spool *last*, you will be pushing the thread through the fabric in the right direction. Your quilting will go more smoothly and you'll have less tangling. Gutermann and YLI hand-quilting threads seem to be the only exceptions to this general rule. Both of these brands are made from Egyptian long-staple cotton which prevents as many hairs from sticking out. The manufacturers have their own secret methods of wrapping the threads and produce the most heavily waxed brands on the market.

Matching the Thread to the Fabric

When I was in high school, I was forced to take Home Economics when I wanted to take Physical Education. I spent the whole semester with an attitude, and, as a result, I did not pay much attention in class. But for some reason, one interesting fact I picked up in Home Economics has stuck with me and it has turned out to be the most valuable piece of information a quilter could possess.

My teacher told me that if we were to make a garment of polyester, we must use polyester thread. If we used silk fabric, we must use silk thread, with cotton we must use cotton thread, and so on. The reason, she said, is that different fibers have different strengths. If you were to make a garment out of polyester and sew it with cotton thread, you would constantly have to re-sew your seams, because the friction of movement would rub one fiber against the other. The polyester would win every time because it is stronger. If you made a garment of cotton and sewed it with polyester thread, the polyester thread would cut the cotton fiber.

In looking at older quilts, I have seen evidence that this "balance of power" between fabric and thread is very important. Quilts made as recently as the 1950s, when polyester first became popular, are already beginning to come back to quilt shops for repairs. In polyester-blend quilts made with cotton threads, the seams need to be re-sewn. In cotton quilts made with polyester threads, cotton patches need to be replaced. My Home Economics teacher was absolutely right! I often wish I had paid better attention in class so that I could have learned a second fact that would help me as a quilter.

Think of the reasons you are making your quilt before you choose your thread. If it is a quilt to fit in with a room decor that might change in a few years anyway, or if it is for a child who will love it to death, matching the thread to the fabric may not be important to you. But if you are making an heirloom quilt or want your quilt to have maximum longevity, take care with thread selection.

Using Silk Thread

Some quilters like to appliqué or do patchwork with silk thread when working with cotton fabrics. They feel that since cotton and silk are both natural fibers, they should be interchangeable. They like the way silk thread seems to glide easily through the layers of fabric. But silk thread is not ideal for quilting anything but silk. Silk has a way of elongating over time and it does not recover very well. This means that a process called *smiling* occurs: seams tend to separate and the stitches produce a sort of laddered look. In other words, it looks like the quilter sewed the pieces together too loosely.

Using Dual-Duty Thread

If polyester is too strong for cotton fabric, then what about quilting thread that has a cotton-wrapped polyester core, such as Coats and Clarks Dual Duty? This thread has not been around long enough to stand the test of time, but it is my opinion that the polyester core will eventually cut through the cotton wrapping and come after your quilt. This will not happen in the 40 years that it takes pure polyester thread to cut through fabric, but it will most likely happen in time. If you are making a quilt you would like your great-grandchildren to enjoy, do not choose dual-duty thread.

Using Metallic Thread

There are many other threads than cotton, polyester, and silk on the market today. Metallic threads are used mostly by machine quilters, but there are a few hand quilters who attempt to use them. It is very difficult to hand quilt with metallic thread because it tangles and frays. If you are determined to use it, I suggest you cut lengths of no more than 12″ (30 cm). Put Fray Chalk—a clear liquid that stabilizes threads

Thread Strength Test
Manufacturers like to claim that their thread is the strongest. This is the number one feature they will point out to quilt shop owners at shows. The funny thing is, they measure strength in units that are meaningless to most of us. Who ever heard of microns of ounces, for example? I conducted a very simple test of threads and found that they are all basically the same strength, waxed or unwaxed. I tied identical lengths of thread to the handle of a small pail, suspended from a rail. I added ounces of sand to the pail until the threads broke. They all broke at about the same weight. The exceptions were metallic and monofilament threads, which obviously carried more weight.

Magic of Summer. Made by Ellen Heck.
This quilting design was inspired by a printed fabric. It was stitched entirely in freehand, without marking the quilting lines. The sun rays are stitched in metallic thread.

from fraying—on your index finger and thumb and pull each length of thread through to coat it or help smooth it down.

Using Sulky Thread

Sulky thread is best described as a ribbon rather than a round thread. It has a tendency to curl up drastically while you are trying to work with it, and it is impossible to control whether it lies flat or on edge. Its strength is not up to par for quilting, either.

Using Invisible Thread

Today, some quilters are using invisible monofilament thread—similar to fishing tackle—for machine appliqué. It was designed so that stitches would not show. Having spent many years on South Pacific islands and on the coast of California, I have a great deal of experience with fishing—I do not personally fish much, but I have always had to contend with tackle boxes all over the garage. I have had the great learning experience of seeing what 10-year-old fishing tackle looks like. It turns yellow and is dry and brittle. Pressing it between your fingers makes it snap more easily than uncooked spaghetti. You might think this weakening is caused by salt water and sunlight, but after examining old spools of tackle on a dark shelf, I found the same thing—yellow, dry, and brittle. Monofilament is a petroleum-based product, and, as such, when open to the air, it oxidizes.

Monofilament quilting thread is exactly the same as fishing tackle, only thinner and even more fragile. Let us hope our children do not have to pick pieces of fine brittle thread from the family heirloom quilt!

Metallic Thread

I once compromised on one of my quilts by using metallic thread for about an eighth of the quilting, just to see how well it worked. I know that that part of the quilt will one day be cut by the thread, and I will live with my decision to experiment. Remember, metallic thread is exactly what it says—metal. It has much greater strength than fabric and will eventually cut your quilt seriously. For this reason, I can never recommend that your family heirloom quilt be quilted in metallic thread.

Quilter's Workshop

Make a fabric sandwich of muslin top, low-loft batting, and muslin backing. Gather together samples of regular sewing thread, waxed quilting thread, unwaxed quilting thread, and an assortment of metallics and monofilament threads. You may even want to run regular thread through beeswax to test that, too. Quilt a little with each thread to compare differences in workability and strength. Look at each thread under a magnifying glass before using and then after it has been pulled through the quilt a few times to observe the wear.

CHAPTER FIVE

Thimbles

When we think of thimbles, many of us remember our mothers or grandmothers sitting quietly and working on a delicate piece of needlework. The first image that comes to mind is of the elegant, lacy sterling silver thimbles they used to shield their fingers from needle puncture. Sterling silver was a sign of quality, and women took care of their thimbles as though they were fine pieces of jewelry. And why not? Those sterling silver thimbles originally cost just as much. Today thimbles come in a variety of shapes and colors. Some are functional; others are strictly collector items. Most quilters have a collection of thimbles that were hoped-for solutions to one source of aggravation or another. We are all searching for the perfect thimble.

Les Sirenes (The Mermaids). Made by Roxanne McElroy.
Waves cover the quilt, and the unique quilted fish scattered throughout add interest. Notice the appliquéd fish on the backing, perfectly stitched to correspond with the quilting design on the quilt top.

The Paddle

Instead of a thimble, some quilters use a little instrument that looks like a tiny tennis racket with a spoon handle attached. House of Quilting's Paddle is simply a dimpled disk with a small handle. It is meant to be held in the hand and the stitches are made by rotating the wrist. It was originally developed to help quilters who, because of arthritis, have difficulty pinching their fingers together to make running stitches. I've tried the Paddle and have worked with it long enough to master the technique, but I found it to be very stressful on my wrist and the back of my hand. At a time when quilters are increasingly concerned about carpel tunnel syndrome, I admit my fears about this tool. Even so, one thing I find annoying is the time wasted with the Paddle—you use it to stack stitches, then you have to put it down while you pull the needle through and reset it, only to pick the Paddle up again to execute the stitches.

How the Muscles in the Quilting Hand Work

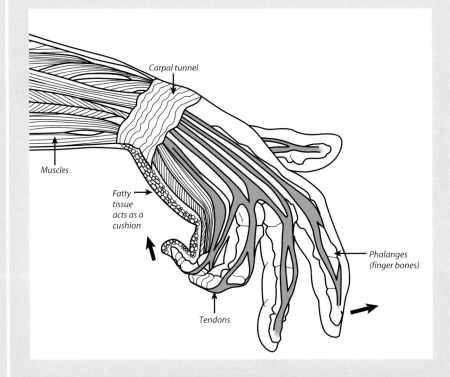

Carpal tunnel

Muscles

Fatty tissue acts as a cushion

Tendons

Phalanges (finger bones)

Because of the muscular-skeletal structure of the hand, it is easy to strain the hand if quilting incorrectly. The term *strain* covers a variety of conditions. Each is caused by constant repetition of a particular hand movement, especially those made under suboptimal conditions and in poor positions. Irritation of the tendons, shown in blue, is a strain that is common among quilters. It is caused by pressure on the median nerve and tendons as they pass through the *carpal tunnel,* a crosswise ligament at the front of the wrist. Tendons and muscles cause bones to move by contracting (shortening) and releasing (returning to normal). Notice the placement of the tendons on the finger bones. They run lengthwise. If you were to pull or contract them near the carpal tunnel, the fingers would move in the direction of the arrows. The human hand does not have muscles that cause the tips of the fingers to move sideways. Quilters who push incorrectly from the side are using a gross motor movement emanating from the carpal tunnel area and the elbow, causing undue strain in those areas as they attempt to control a highly skilled action such as the quilting stitch. Quilters who have been forced to use the very tip of their fingers due to poorly shaped thimbles are jamming the finger joints. This can cause early forms of arthritis and can certainly aggravate preexisting conditions.

Choosing a Thimble

Needlework thimbles, like the ones our grandmothers wore, are not at all suited to the art of quilting for many reasons. Most have walls too thin to withstand the extreme pressure required to penetrate the multiple layers of a quilt. When there are four very tiny stitches already on the needle and the quilter is trying for a fifth, the pressure on the needle is enormous! Pushing a needle through all those tiny stitches is very hard on a thimble with thin walls. The quilter is in grave danger of being wounded.

So what should a quilter look for when selecting a thimble? I have spent a great deal of time and effort searching for thimbles and evaluating them. I would like to share my findings with you to help you make the right choice.

Evaluating Thimble Dimples

The size and depth of the dimples on the outside of a thimble play an important part in quilting. This is because the dimples affect your control of the needle, and for That Perfect Stitch, absolute control is critical. If the blunt end of the needle has to slide around searching for a sparsely placed dimple, control is impossible. Similarly, if the needle slips out of a dimple that is too shallow or catches on one that is too deep, control is lost. One thimble, the Carol Bradley thimble, has dimples that are much too deep and the needle catches at such an angle that it breaks off at the eye!

Minimizing Stress on the Fingers

My research into thimbles led me to an orthopedic surgeon for an in-depth study of anatomy. I learned how important it is to choose a thimble that allows us to push the needle through the layers of a quilt *at the correct angle*. Our finger joints actually act as shock absorbers. The bone ends are covered with cartilage and, when working properly, form a sealed container for the vital fluids that lubricate the cartilage and so lessen the friction when we use or bend our fingers. Our fingers are meant to bend only one way. Repeated pressure to the side of a joint—which happens when a needle is pushed at an incorrect

Comparing Thimbles

Flat-top thimbles force you to push . . .

. . . with the top of a finger, like this.

A well-designed thimble allows you to push . . .

. . . with the ball and pad of the finger, like this . . .

Not from the top, like this . . .

. . . and not sideways, like this.

Return to M'Zima, Waiting for the Rain. Made by Patricia Harrington, Spring, TX.

The background quilting follows the curved piecing to accent the movement—of seasons and of the animals.
The rest of the quilting accents the animals moving toward the springs at M'Zima in the center. The quilter used
an overlay of a piece of black fabric, then placed the animals, and cut the black fabric away as she appliquéd.

angle—will eventually result in irritation to the joint and can lead to premature arthritis. One form of arthritis is caused by loss of lubrication in the joints. The bone ends rub against each other, causing irritation and inflammation.

There are several thimbles on the market that have ridged flap tops. All of these are faulty in design because they cause the quilter to use the tip of the finger—rather than the ball and pad of the finger—to push the needle. The muscles in the finger simply do not work in this direction. It is an extremely stressful angle, not to mention inefficient for quilting. Flat-top thimbles usually have a grid of dimples at the top, but in an effort to gain more control over the needle and to protect the finger, most quilters rely on the ridge around the top to catch the needle. This causes the thimble to cant, giving the quilter calluses around the finger where the edge of the thimble rubs.

Evaluating Thimble Strength

Most thimbles are not built for the strength it takes to push the needle through the layers of a quilt. The Tailors Thimble is one of these. What I do like about it, though, is the protection it affords. Designed in China hundreds of years ago, The Tailors Thimble is made up of a band of metal with dimples that slides on around the finger to protect the ball or pad.

The weakest thimbles I have found are made of leather. And, because they lack strength, these are the most dangerous types of thimble to use. Leather simply cannot withstand the pressures the better quilters exert, and needles puncture quilting fingers regularly. A leather thimble will only last a good quilter about a month, and comparatively speaking, they are very expensive. Some manufacturers, in an effort to increase the life span of leather thimbles, insert a metal pad into the leather. What happens, though, is that because this metal plate is

Plastic Thimbles

You may have come across little plastic thimbles that are often given away by manufacturers promoting other products. Because the dimples on these are too shallow, they are not practical as quilting tools at all. Moreover, they are not strong enough to withstand the pressure on the needle, which when pushed forcefully can penetrate them.

smooth, the needle point slides to the edge of it and right off into the fingers. The one benefit of a leather thimble is that the quilter can avoid joint damage by using the ball of the finger properly.

Thimbles and Fingernails

My next stop in researching thimbles was a Beauty School to consult with a fingernail expert. Many women today choose to wear long nails or artificial nails. The simple act of drumming the nails on a table causes shock waves to travel up through the nail bed to the root of the nail. When pushing a thimble, the pressure is much greater. If the trauma is heavy enough, the nail grows out with ridges across it. At the very least, the nail becomes brittle or weak and tends to break or split easily, making it difficult for women to achieve a well manicured look. Being crammed repeatedly into a thimble also cuts off oxygen to the nail, adding to this condition.

I have come across a soft gray rubber thimble, designed to accommodate long fingernails. It has a slanted top that is gridded. The thimble works well to push the needle through the layers of the quilt, but when you release the pressure to grab the needle, you often find that the needle has stuck into the thimble, pulling the stitches back out!

Even if you are not concerned about keeping long or well manicured nails, keep in mind that even short nails get jammed inside flat-top thimbles, causing discomfort and making it difficult to stitch.

Thimble Size

The single most frustrating problem with the thimbles on the market is that most of them come in a limited size range. When I could not find a thimble to fit me, even a bad thimble, I had to resort to leather ones. Leather thimbles restrict movement—it feels as though you are trying to quilt with a glove on. And, as we have seen, they are simply not strong enough for quilting.

A thimble I thought would be pretty good was one made of plastic with an open front. The open front accommodated long fingernails, and the dimples were nice and deep. Unfortunately, this thimble comes in only two or three sizes, none of which fit me. I was told to put it in a pan of boiling water. This would supposedly soften the plastic enough to adjust the fit. I tried a couple of times and I could not get it to work. Either nothing at all happened or the thimble ended up a blob of plastic in the bottom of my pan. That is probably my fault though—I cook like that, too.

Roxanne's Thimble

My research into thimbles over several years left me feeling frustrated and my fingers feeling sore. I even began to be embarrassed that my fingers were too big for almost all the thimbles on the market. I was forced to find a solution to my problem if I wanted to continue quilting. The first thing I did was to set my own criteria for the ultimate thimble. I wanted a thimble that was big enough for me, but would not fall off or rotate around my finger. I wanted to be able to push with the ball of my finger, not the tip. Since the ball of the finger is rounded, the dimples had to be deep enough to control my needle as I moved it from a 90° angle to a 180° angle without having to put my thumb on it. It had to be strong, open in front to protect the nail, and pretty to wear. Since I was going to so much trouble, I also wanted my thimble to last me the rest of my life! The product is called Roxanne's Thimble, and comes in fifteen different sizes—the smallest on the market to the largest on the market. It is shown in the photograph on page 35.

The most important thing in choosing a thimble is that it not budge on your finger at all, not cause joint stress, and allow for complete needle control. Without these features, it is impossible to obtain That Perfect Stitch.

Quilter's Workshop

Try on thimbles in varying sizes to find the one that is right for you. Make sure that it is comfortable, but that it does not fall off easily or rotate on your finger. Take a small "quilt sandwich" of batting, backing, and quilt top with you to the store and try out the thimble you think fits best.

CHAPTER SIX

Frames and Hoops

We realized very early in our quilt history that it was beneficial to keep the layers of the quilt taut during the quilting process in order to avoid pleats and puckers in the finished work. There was a variety of ways to do this but generally it involved building some kind of frame. The quilter would fasten together strips of wood the size of the piece to be quilted. The slats were about 1″ (2.5 cm) thick, 2″ (5 cm) wide, and up to 108″ (275 cm) long. Each slat had a narrow strip of fabric nailed or stapled to it onto which the edges of the quilt backing were basted. This method required heavy basting and often provided a social occasion, where women would gather for a meal and help a friend baste her quilt, who in turn would join in the basting of another's quilt.

Gingko. Made by Roxanne McElroy.
Notice how the basting stitches radiate from the center. The quilt top is based on a Japanese family crest design that is more than a thousand years old. The quilt is photographed in the Grace Frame. The quilt in the hoop, above, Ia Orana by Dierdra McElroy, uses outline quilting of a pattern in the fabric onto the white muslin background.

Space Savers!

I once heard a fascinating story of early quilters and their frames. To save space, a quilter would suspend her frame from the ceiling by hooks and pulleys so she could raise it when it was not in use. This was usually done over dining tables or beds because of the space required for a quilt frame of such dimensions. It is a very exciting image for me to think of looking up from my table or bed to see the back of my current quilt-in-progress! I have often fantasized about installing a frame this way, but it would probably be for sake of conversation only. I tend to lean heavily on my quilt frame and would be in grave danger of knocking a hole in a wall or breaking a window!

C-Clamp Frames

Since the earliest days of quilting, frames have not really changed much. They were typically made of 1″ × 4″ (2.5 cm × 10 cm) lengths of wood. The wood was put together in almost the exact dimensions of the quilt itself and then held together with C-clamps (metal tools shaped like the letter C with a foot that screws down onto another foot, securing two objects together). The quilt top, batting, and backing were put together and then placed over the frame and tacked down to the poles. There was no basting to be done, which is a big advantage, but this type of frame took up phenomenal amounts of space. Imagine a king size quilt laid out flat in your living room! Frames like this are still fairly common, since many quilters can sit around them, stitching together. A disadvantage is that the quilting is done from the outside in, which can cause irreversible puckers at the center of the quilt if the quilters are not careful.

Installing the Quilt

When using a traditional C-clamp frame, enlist the help of friends to install the quilt.

1. The pole dimensions should be no larger or slightly smaller than the quilt dimensions. Measure from the outside of one pole to the outside of the other pole when the frame is assembled.
2. Put the poles together and secure the joints with C-clamps.
3. Spread the backing over the frame face down, making sure it is square and not distorted. Tack it to the frame with quilting thumb tacks.
4. Next, place the batting over the frame making sure an equal amount of batting is hanging over each edge. It is best to make your batting slightly larger than the quilt itself, since the quilting process will shrink it slightly. You can either tack it down with new tacks or, if you have helpers, remove the first tacks one by one from the backing and place them over the batting and backing.
5. Finally the top goes on face up. Center it and tack it down to the frame. The frame can then either be placed on stanchions (stands), or suspended from the ceiling.

Basting

The quilt can either be basted before going into the frame, in which case all three layers are tucked onto the frame simultaneously, or it can be basted after installation. If the quilt is not basted, do not remove it from the frame until it is completely quilted. If you choose to baste first, the best way to baste is from the center out, thus drawing the wrinkles out to the edges to be released. Make a basting line from the center out to each side of the quilt, then baste from the center out to each corner. From here, continue basting lines from center out running between the lines already done. Personally I wouldn't leave more than 3″ (8 cm) between basting lines radiating outward.

Sawhorse Frames

Another basic type of frame that has been traditionally used by quilters is the sawhorse frame. This frame is more widely used than the one described above because it is easy to make and takes up less space. Similar in construction to the sawhorses carpenters use, the frame is a little taller—36″ (90 cm) rather than 28″ (70 cm). Two sawhorses are set up opposite each other and 2″ × 2″ (5 cm × 5 cm) quilt poles are nestled into notches cut into the crossbars, equidistant from one another. The length of the poles vary depending on the size of the quilt to be worked on. The tension on the quilt is limited to one turn of the pole. Quilters can sit together on either side of the frame and, when finished working for the day, the poles can be lifted out of the sawhorses, rolled up together, and stored in a closet until the next session.

Basting and Installing the Quilt

This is a primitive frame that requires heavy basting before the quilt is put into the frame. When using a two-pole sawhorse system, the best method is to baste as you roll the quilt into the frame. This way, the quilt gets basted without the space required to lay it flat.

1. Mark the center of the back pole by measuring the length and then dividing that length in half. Find the center of your quilt backing by folding it in half lengthwise. Pin the center of the quilt backing to the muslin strip attached to your pole at its center spot. Gently smooth and pin the backing to the muslin strip, starting at the center point and working out. When you finish one side it might be wise to measure from where the fabric ends to the end of the pole. Make sure that same distance is left on the other side after it is pinned and before the backing is basted down. Once the backing is attached to

Quick Baste

Some quilters have come up with ingenious ways to baste their quilts into frames. One quilter I know insists it is less work basting the layers of a quilt together if the frame is laid across the seats of chairs. She lays down on the floor underneath the frame and bastes it! Another quilter stands the quilt frame up in a wide doorway and recruits a friend to stand on the back side of the quilt to grab the basting needle and direct it back through to the front of the quilt! Both quilters claim their methods serve to avoid back pain. Personally, I agree the most painless way to baste a quilt is to stand the frame in a doorway. But I would prefer to recruit two friends to stand on either side of the frame to baste, while I supervise with a glass of Coke and a lap full of appliqué!

King Kamehameha. Made by Roxanne McElroy.

Here the sun is accentuated with diagonal rays. The body is echo-quilted to give it an inward energy.

the pole and centered, you can baste it to the muslin strip and remove the straight pins.

2. Repeat Step 1 with the opposite side of the quilt backing. Make sure that the same distances are kept from the fabric edge to the ends of the poles. Baste securely after pinning and measuring.

3. Roll the quilt backing onto the back pole until the center of the backing is reached. (The easiest way to find these center points is to fold the fabric or batting in half lengthwise, then in half crosswise. The center fold is also the center point. Temporarily mark them.) It is vital that you watch the fabric on the poles as you roll. The overlapping edges must be right on top of each other with edges matching.

4. Repeat Step 3 but roll the backing onto the front pole. Again watch the edges as they overlap onto the pole; they should match exactly. If they do not you need to re-baste the backing to the pole and measure carefully.

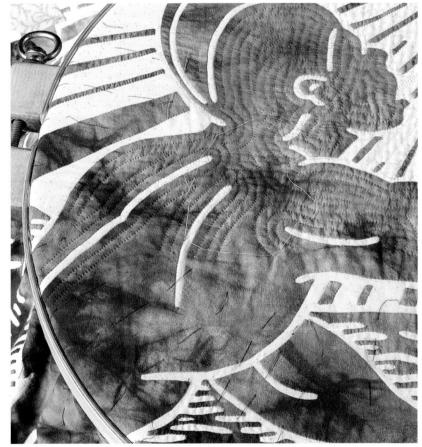

5. Drape the batting over the quilt frame with the center point of batting matching the center point of the quilt backing. (It can be very helpful, depending on the batting you choose, to remove the batting from its package and lay it out flat over a bed or on the floor overnight to let the wrinkles settle.)

6. Drape the quilt top over the quilt frame with the center point matching the center points of the batting and backing.

7. Begin basting the quilt at the center point. Smooth the top flat and baste using a very long needle and any cotton thread. Run a line of basting stitches to each edge from the center always

working outward. Continue running basting lines across the quilt, mindful of quilt edges as they roll. Begin quilting at the center working out. Continue running basting lines across the quilt from the center out every 3″ (8 cm) until you get very close to a pole. Then, roll the basted part of the quilt onto the pole, exposing new areas to quilt. As you roll, make sure the edges of the quilt overlap exactly, to ensure the quilt is basted squarely. Once half the quilt is basted, roll it back to the center carefully, and work on the other half from the center out.

Take care not to roll the quilt into the frame too tightly. If the quilt is "drum-tight," you have no room at all to warp the layers over the needle to achieve That Perfect Stitch and you may be inadvertently warping the squareness of your quilt.

Three-Pole Frames

The three-pole frame was first introduced about 75 years ago. In a good three-pole system there is no need for basting. The quilt top and batting are rolled together onto one pole; the backing is rolled onto a second pole; and the whole quilt is then pulled forward and wrapped around the front pole. Basting has always been one of my least favorite things to do, so you can imagine my excitement upon discovering the three-pole system years ago. The Grace Company makes a frame known as the Grace Frame (see page 42) in which the designer has added even a fourth pole option! This way, both the top and batting each have their own separate poles. With this quilting system a quilt will always lay perfectly flat upon completion!

Choosing a Frame

There are several frames on the market and some can mean a serious investment in your quilting. Before you make that investment do your homework!

Height

A quilt frame should be high enough that when your upper arm is at the side of your body, and your forearm is extended out, the pole of the frame fits right into the bend of the arm. Some frames have a tilt feature that might help tailor the height to your body. Another option is to use a good quality orthopedic, height adjustable chair. Adjust the chair to your frame for posture and comfort. The tilt feature can oftentimes provide an easier angle for more comfortable quilting than bending over at a 90° angle.

Tension

A quilt should never be put into a frame drum-tight. That Perfect Stitch can only be achieved when the fabric is loose enough to manipulate around your needle. You will quickly discover that adjusting the tension on your frame in fine degrees is a valuable feature. To achieve an even tension along the length of the poles a ratchet system is most effective. This takes out the "human factor" of hand-rotating your poles. The larger the diameter of the ratchets, the finer the degree of tensioning available.

Sturdiness

My number one requirement of a quilting frame is sturdiness. As I have said, I tend to lean heavily on my frame as I quilt and it makes me very unhappy to feel the frame giving way under my weight. Norwood and Hinterburg make frames so beefy an elephant could sit on them. Made from solid oak, but available in other woods, these frames are so thick that the poles themselves must also be thick in order to give them a balanced look. I found this truly beautiful frame to be uncomfortable because of the pole thicknesses. Once the quilt is wrapped onto the poles the overall diameter is then too large to reach an arm under comfortably to begin quilting. I have to wonder if this would cause back or neck problems in the long term.

The Grace Frame, photographed at the beginning of this chapter, is particularly sturdy. Another feature I like about it is that the poles are laminated rather than made of solid wood. This prevents them from bowing with age, which renders them useless. Most frames come with poles of varying lengths to accommodate quilts of different sizes. The Grace Frame comes instead with short extensions to a single set of poles that interlock for strength. No more long poles laying around the garage!

Size

Since most of us do not have an entire room dedicated to our quilting, space is always an important consideration when choosing a full-size frame. Standard frames measure 34″ (86 cm) deep, but some are available in a narrow-profile that only measures 28″ (70 cm). If you are going to be the only one quilting at the frame (versus group quilting),

Fish Schools. Made by Judy Hopkins, San Diego, CA.

Notice the use of different quilt designs for different blocks.

then the narrow profile is a more efficient use of space. After all, there is only just so far that your arms can reach across the frame and the rest is dead space. Some frames dismantle quickly for space but I have to say that in my experience you are kidding yourself if you think that you will put up a frame "just long enough to get this quilt done" and then take it down! Every single hand quilter I have talked to admits that her frame has become a part of her decor. My biggest piece of advice to you would be to shop for a frame as you would a piece of furniture. Require the same functionality as well as beauty from your frame that you would look for in a sofa or dining table.

Quilting Hoops

A full-size quilt frame with a ratcheting system and three poles is the ideal quilting system. Unfortunately, not all quilters have the ways or means to place a large frame in their homes. In other words, a compromise is in order. I use a hoop to quilt all my small pieces and find it very convenient for my busy lifestyle. Many quilters choose to use hoops because they can be rotated in order always to quilt in a favorite direction. Others choose them because they want to quilt in the same room with their families.

Mounted Hoops

Several companies offer hoops mounted on stands. Some are mounted on lap stands and others are on floor stands, making them taller. These types of hoops not only make great display pieces for any room, they allow you to keep quite a bit of the quilt off your lap while you work. They take up much less space than a full-size frame, and they can usually be rotated to many directions to facilitate quilting.

When searching for a hoop-on-a-stand, be sure that there is sufficient space under the hoop between the stand and where your quilt would be. Often, I have found the space to be limited, making quilting more difficult as you maneuver around the stand. Rotation in conjunction with tilt is a very handy feature, allowing the quilter to better position the hoop for That Perfect Stitch. However, many rotating hoops have one spot that will not tilt when rotated in that direction and that can be very frustrating. Jasmine Heirlooms has an incredible one called the Easy Spinner Hoop Stand, photographed on page 46. The hoop is mounted on a ball joint allowing it to tilt and rotate at all angles. The stand itself also tilts from a 90° angle to flat on

Beauty

My motto has always been "Beauty in Form and Function." The two must go hand in hand and one is useless without the other. Jasmine Heirlooms makes a three-pole frame that is stunning in beauty. It has scroll-worked legs and a beautiful stain. Do not let beauty be the main indication of function. This frame is closer to a sawhorse design. Norwood and Hinterburg's frames are darkly stained and very beautiful. The Grace Company can stain your new frame any shade you would like to match your decor or it can come to you unfinished if you would like to stain it yourself. Pleasant Mountain also makes a beautiful upper-end frame that runs a close second to the Grace Frame in functionality.

Lap Quilting

Georgia Bonesteel gets my MVP award for single-handedly making the quilting process portable. She developed a method of quilting called *lap quilting*, which is done by quilting one good size square at a time and then attaching the quilted squares together with French-Feld seams. This method convinced quilters that they could do entire quilts in a hoop, and it was a huge stepping stone to portability for all of us.

the floor, allowing you to raise or lower the overall head to match the chair you are sitting in. The drawback is its cost. You will spend almost as much for this stand as you would for a basic full-size quilt frame.

Some hoops are mounted on lap stands making them portable and lightweight. The stand takes the weight of the hoop and quilt off your underneath hand, making it easier to achieve That Perfect Stitch.

A couple of companies manufacture small "frames" about the size of a card table. These are really just big hoops on legs. They require heavy basting and careful placement in the hoop. The PVC plastic floor "frame" is convenient for groups that travel, since it dismantles quickly. However, never leave a quilt in it while not working. The plastic can stretch and eventually will no longer hold tightly. Also, don't leave this hoop in the trunk of your car on a hot summer day—it will suffer major melt-down!

Hand-Held Hoops

I have seen quilters go to their local quilting bees with a bed-size quilt dumped into a laundry basket. They have a 14" (35 cm) or 16" (40 cm) hoop in one area of the quilt that they lift out and work on! It obviously works for them. The disadvantage to this system is that you are always stuck with lots of quilt in your lap that could get quite warm, depending on where you live and the time of year. Trying to rotate the hoop can also be quite cumbersome.

Round Hoops

Most wooden hoops are about the same. Some are prettier than others, and they vary in diameter. I find the 14" (35 cm) hoop to be the most functional, but experiment with 12" (30 cm) and 16" (40 cm) hoops to see which is most comfortable for you. Some companies, such as Norwood, make a "bungee cord" hoop. A stretchable bungee cord is wrapped around one layer of a round hoop. The advantage is that the hoop helps avoid stark creases in the fabric; a disadvantage is that it does not hold the quilt as tightly as traditional hoops.

There is a fiberglass hoop on the market that uses a system of rubber bands to keep the quilt firmly in place. This is the No-Slip Hoop by Elliott Morgan. The problem is that the bands make it impossible to budge the quilt once it is placed in the hoop. This means that if the quilt is positioned in the hoop with a distortion that is not at first noticeable, the quilter will be unable to adjust the tension in the hoop and will have no choice but to quilt right over the problem spot.

Square Hoops

Square hoops, usually made from pvc plastic, are extremely compact and portable. Because the hoop is square, the quilter automatically places the quilt in it with the grain lines perfectly straight, thus avoiding distortions. A disadvantage, however, is that there are four awkward corners to quilt around. As you turn the hoops to quilt in your favorite direction, it is impossible to avoid poking yourself in the tummy with a corner. The sides of square hoops adjust independently of each other and tend to be quite tight. I worry that this makes it too easy to distort the quilt. Never leave your quilt in a square hoop when not in use. The plastic clamps can stretch, so removing them will increase your hoop's longevity.

Placing the Quilt in a Hoop

The danger of quilting a large quilt in a hoop is the risk of distorting it. I am sure you have seen, more times than you care to remember, quilts on which the bottom edges are rippled and wavy. That distortion can only occur in two ways: either the quilter was not careful with her hoop while quilting, or she did not use a hoop or frame at all!

You see, the most wonderful thing about fabric is its stretchability and the most awful thing about fabric is . . . its stretchability. Piecers love the straight of the grain and curse the bias. Appliquérs adore the bias and have to be very careful when working with the straight of the grain. A hand quilter must beware of the bias, not because it is difficult to quilt on, but because it is so easy to inadvertently distort your quilt in the hoop by pulling on the bias while adjusting it. Distortions are quilted in and the quilt will not relax back to its original shape.

When you are putting a quilt into a hoop, if you should have a little pucker, do not pull on a bias corner to straighten it! Instead, pull gently with the straight of the grain to the north or south, east or west. Never pull diagonally. Pulling on the grain will tighten and flatten the quilt in the hoop without distorting it.

To further avoid distortions, heavy basting is a must. Begin by running basting lines from the center out to each edge, then run basting lines from the center to each corner. Depending on the size of the quilt, keep running basting lines from the center out until no more than 3″ (8 cm) is left unbasted between the radiating lines.

CHAPTER SEVEN

Markers

When I had been a quilter for several years, my aunt called me to tell me that we have a family heirloom quilt. It was made in 1930 by my grandmother and my aunts. Until that day, I had not been aware that anyone in my family had ever quilted! My aunt told me that she would send the quilt to me—to clean it for her. I decided that if this quilt had been kept that big a secret, I should accept the offer or I might never get to see it. When the box arrived, I carefully opened it. Tears came to my eyes when I saw what had happened. The lines of the quilting design had been marked onto the quilt top with the newest writing utensil to come to my grandmother's tiny Kansas farming community: ball-point pen. The lines were as bright a blue as the day they were marked.

Tahitian Hibiscus. Made by Roxanne McElroy.
With a simple crosshatch design, this miniature whole-cloth quilt demonstrates that, with practice, the stitches on the top and on the back and the spaces on the top and on the back can be exactly the same length. It is shown on top of a wonderful white-on-white quilt, **Circles,** *by Hazel Canny.*

Springtime over Baltimore. Made by Anita Askins.
The white satin flowers are made from scraps left over from making a
wedding dress, which the quilter sewed for her daughter. This fabric is
reminiscent of the white silk used in antique album quilts.

Choosing Markers

This sad story serves to show that what most of us would think is the easiest item to select for quilting has proven to be the toughest. The lesson to be learned is that *any* marking utensil should be tested. Just because it is new on the market and even if it claims to be designed for quilting, don't take chances with any marking utensil until you know for sure it will not damage your quilt.

Markers are used to transfer the lines of a quilting design onto a quilt top so that it can be quilted. The goal is to find a marker that transfers onto the top with little effort, will stay on until all the quilting is done, and comes off afterward without leaving any chemicals or residue behind to damage the fibers of the quilt. It is important to test *all* marking tools for removability on *all* fabrics in the quilt top *before* the top is marked. This is the only way to assure yourself your quilt will be safe.

Pens

There are a couple of marking pens on the market I feel compelled to warn against. Dritz and EZ make pens that are supposed to magically disappear in 12 hours. One brand is touted to quilters as "the purple

pen that vanishes." I had the pen analyzed by a chemist. The base chemical in this type of pen erodes the fibers of fabric, and, even though the color may disappear right away, the chemical is still there. My analyst also indicated that purple seems to be the only color that adheres to that particular chemical.

One day I was visiting a quilt shop in Texas when an hysterical woman came into the shop with a bundle in her arms— a quilt she had finished two years before. She held part of the quilt between her hands with a line of quilting between her thumbs and gently pulled. The quilt top fabric

Marker Test

I examined several different types of markers and evaluated them in terms of ease of movement over fabric, washability, and flexibility in marking a variety of colors and prints. On a scale of 1 to 10 (1 is poor, 10 is excellent), I assigned a rating to each. Here are my results.

Berol silver/white chalk	9
Roxanne's Quilter's Choice	10
Soapstone marker	7
Blue pens that wash out	2
Purple pens that vanish	1
#2 pencils	2
Anita Shackelford's graphite marker	5
Ultimate marking pencil	4
Chalk pouncers	5

All ratings are based on my personal examinations of products I have used

tore away along the quilting stitches as if the fabric were a piece of perforated paper. The chemicals in the purple pen that vanishes had actually eaten the fabric along the lines where it was originally marked.

Dritz also makes a blue marking pen that stays on until removed with a damp sponge. My chemist told me the chemicals in this pen are very strong and the only color that can adhere to them is blue. Wiping with a damp sponge is not enough to rid the quilt of the blue color. If not actually soaked in water for some time, the blue color tends to sink down through the quilt top and into the batting. It has a tendency to resurface again and again.

Even if the blue color does go, this does not mean the chemicals are gone as well. There are instances, not always, but enough times to raise concerns, where the chemicals have come back permanently as a dirty brown line. I've been told that the company response has been that the quilter had the quilt dry cleaned or ironed the quilt top after marking the quilting lines. Even if this is so, I could never recommend a pen with chemicals that so dramatically shorten the life of a quilt.

Soap and Chalk

Soap slivers and chalk are good markers, but they rub off the fabric very easily. This means you should not mark much ahead of yourself. Chalk pencils are safe only when in their two naturally occuring colors—gray/silver or white. Beware of chalk pencils that are yellow, red, or green. These colors are dyes and may not come out.

Pencils

The most basic marking tool is, of course, the common pencil. The graphite in pencils, commonly referred to as the lead, comes in many different hardnesses. The softer the graphite, the more residue rubs off onto the fabric fibers. Harder graphites are more difficult to see on fabric since they leave less residue, and, as a result, quilters tend to press much harder with them, forcing the graphite into the fibers. When this happens, it becomes even more difficult than softer graphite to get out of the fabric. Graphite is particularly problematic on painted fabric. More and more we are seeing quilts in which the graphite has not washed out of the painted parts of the fabric.

Many otherwise perfect quilts have lead pencil marks that remain to detract from their beauty. The appraised value of a quilt is affected by these marks and new quilts in competition are eliminated if the marks show.

The silver Berol pencil marks very well, stays on long enough to quilt the whole thing, and then washes out. Its only disadvantage is that it is very delicate, and many quilters report wasting half the pencil trying to sharpen it to a point.

I found a pencil, however, that surpasses anything I have yet used. As a matter of fact, I liked the pencil so much that I bought the company that makes it. That way, I would be assured an unending supply. The pencil, Quilter's Choice, comes in silver or white. It is a little softer than Berol so it marks with a little less force. It also needs to be sharpened less and holds a point very well, as it has an organic compound that stops excessive crumbling. Quilter's Choice is photographed at the beginning of this chapter.

Do Not Tap Pencils!

If you tap a pencil against a table it breaks the lead inside the wood and you will never get it sharpened. That is why using pencils as drumsticks is not a good idea. This is especially true with delicate chalk pencils. Simply dropping it onto your sewing table can cause the core lead to break.

Quilter's Workshop

1. Choose a variety of fabrics and marking utensils. Mark each fabric with each marker. Allow to sit for a period of time and then wash. Note the marker, the method of washing, and the type of soap on the back of each piece of fabric. Observe the marks on each fabric and draw conclusions based on the marker and type of fabric.

2. Repeat the exercise above, but this time subject fabrics to different conditions before washing. Be sure to note the types of conditions tested on the back of each piece of fabric. Test the effects of ironing, storage under fluorescent lights, storage in a dark closet, and erasing markings with a soft eraser.

CHAPTER EIGHT

Other Helpful Aids

Over the years, quilters have used the most unexpected tools to help them with their quilting. We are lucky that today there are products on the market for virtually every need we may have. There are still a few unconventional items, however, that at first seem out of place in a sewing kit, but that no serious quilter would be without. Necessity is the mother of invention. I encourage you as a quilter to invent when necessary. All too often quilters blame their lack of expertise or dexterity for any problems they encounter while hand quilting. When you run into a problem, ask "why" first. Analyze the collection of products you are using in the quilt to determine what is going wrong. Then find a way to fix it. No rights or wrongs if it works for you!

Scottish Thistle. Made by Roxanne McElroy.

Quilting along the dividing lines of plaid fabric can give the illusion of a pieced background.

Orangutan. Made by Nancy S. Brown, Outland, CA.

Background quilting is done in a crazy quilt pattern. Most of the other quilting follows the natural lines of the orangutan, leaves, and trees.

Protecting Your Fingers

Once you have mastered That Perfect Stitch, you will have no sore fingers at all. However, while you are learning to coordinate your movements, you will sometimes get them out of sequence and will end up with a few needle pricks on your fingers. Generally, I do not recommend using anything underneath the quilt because it is imperative to feel the needle in order to stop pushing in time. A few quilters have fingers so sensitive that they need to use something, however. Jasmine's Needle Glider or Aunt Becky's thimble are two viable options.

Within a couple of days of beginning to quilt, a callus should form to help protect your finger. In the meantime, there is a product in almost all pharmacies that will help. New Skin comes in liquid form or convenient spray. A couple of coats on the finger you use to balance the point of the needle under the quilt will provide a thin protective coating between your finger and the needle. Be absolutely certain the product is dry before touching your quilt, however, because it does contain a very strong chemical. Once dry it just peels or washes off.

You can also buy tape specifically designed to protect the fingers from needle pricks. I hesitate to use any kind of tape, however, that will be near my needle point because tape residue always adheres to the needle and a build-up causes drag. Additionally, muting the feeling of the underneath finger often hinders a quilter from learning when to push and when to stop pushing.

If your poor fingers are absolute hamburger and yet you have a deadline on the quilt because that baby is going to be born any day now, then I suggest you run down to your local supermarket and buy the cheapest pair of unlined gloves you can find. Cut a finger off the glove and put it on the finger under the quilt. It is true you may end up with tiny bits of rubber stuck to the back of your quilt, but that is infinitely better than shedding blood. Do not use thick rubber page turners because the rubber is too thick. It is impossible to back the needle out with each stitch.

If you are considering using a cream on your callused finger, be sure you choose the correct one for your problem. Bag Balm is popular, and you can find it at most quilt shops. It is also available from feed supply stores—a can will last you and a few hundred of your closest friends for life! Designed to soften the udders of cows and prevent infection when nursing, Bag Balm is somewhat greasy. A less greasy version is Udder Cream. Both contain softeners and antiseptics. They do nothing for the pain if your finger is sore.

Sore Fingers

If you are on a deadline and your finger is getting too sore to sew, I have a sure overnight cure: Preparation H. As well as softener and antiseptic, it contains a mild analgesic for pain.

Spring Garden.
Made by Margaret Illion,
Las Vegas, NV.
Sometimes crosshatching is the appropriate thing to do!

Taking Care of the Quilter's Callus

It is very important to gain a callus to help protect your finger. Take care, however, that the callus does not thicken to the point that it is impossible to feel the needle coming through the layers of the quilt. Use an emery board to file down the callus to a manageable thickness.

Every night before you retire, you should rub your callus with Bag Balm lotion or Udder Cream salve. Since these products were originally developed by veterinarians to keep the udders of cows soft and supple, they will do the same for your finger.

Protecting Your Eyes

I urge you to see your ophthalmologist before you get heavily into quilting. Most doctors automatically make you a prescription for a reading distance of 18" (46 cm). We can easily move a book to the right distance to read, but that is not the case with quilting. Take your quilting with you to the doctor and demonstrate how you sit to quilt. Your doctor will gladly make your prescription right for you.

If you cannot thread your needle in a couple of tries, then I suggest you use a needle threader. Why waste your eyes on something as simple as that when you will need your expert eyesight to see the tiny stitches you will be making?

Aids for Faster Quilting

Once we find our special rhythm, it is upsetting to stop and pull the needle through all the fine stitches we stacked on the needle.

Sometimes we hate so much to stop that we find we actually put so many stitches on the needle we can no longer pull the needle through at all. This is where the Needle Grabbit comes in handy. Keep it lying on your hoop and when you need it you can pick it up by pinching the center of the rubber between forefinger and thumb. Then, simply grab the needle and pull it through.

Some quilters use forceps to do the same thing. I cannot recommend using forceps unless they are rubber coated, as they tend to strip the plating off the needle. This will cost you time and frustration.

A very popular item to use is the finger cot. Roll it down your finger to help get a good grip on the needle to pull it through the layers. The finger cot is especially helpful for quilters with arthritis, when gripping causes pain. It is also a good time-saver, since there is no picking up or putting down to do. If you cannot get hold of a finger cot, you could snip the tips of penny balloons and use these instead. They do not provide as good a fit as finger cots, but they do come in pretty colors!

CHAPTER NINE

The Quilting Stitch

As you will find out, the quilting stitch is quite intricate, involving a sequence of precise finger movements. For a lucky few, it takes just a few minutes to learn. For others, it feels awkward and takes a few hours' practice. But when you get it right, it is like being hit by a thunderbolt. Perfect stitches soon become second nature—nothing looks or feels better. Nothing, that is, except the sheer joy of completing your own beautiful handmade quilt. Hand quilting, when done properly, is relaxing, soothing, and satisfying. There should be no pain in the arm, hand, or shoulder or underneath your fingers. Once you master That Perfect Stitch, you will create amazing works of art.

Circles. Made by Hazel Canny.
This incredible white-on-white quilt demonstrates exquisite stitches in a trapunto design.
The quilt above is **Hummingbirds,** *made by Dierdra McElroy.*

Front and Back

For That Perfect Stitch, the stitches on the back of the quilt should be as close as possible in size to those on the front. This takes practice, but it is not impossible. On some of my best quilts, the stitches on the back are identical in size to the stitches on the front. On *Tahitian Hibiscus* (see page 54), for example, the front and the back are indistinguishable. You can tell if your quilting is even if the stitches on the front and back of the quilt and the spaces on the front and back of the quilt are exactly the same length.

Threading the Needle

If you look at a piece of thread through a strong magnifying glass or a microscope, you will clearly see the *knap*, its featherlike surface (see page 29). Every time thread is pulled through fabric, the knap wears a little thinner and the thread gradually weakens. To minimize this, cut thread to a length of no more than 18″ (46 cm). This also helps avoid tangles when quilting. Better yet, use Gutermann or YLI quilting thread because they have no knap at all.

If you are using a thread with a knap, such as Metler by Metrosene, make sure you pull the thread through the fabric in the right direction. Pulling against the knap is like pulling a feather through a tiny hole against its natural grain. How can you tell which way the knap lies? Since knap is a result of the way in which thread was wrapped onto the spool in the factory, the answer is easy: simply remember always to knot the end of the thread that comes off the spool *last*! If you are planning several hours of quilting at one time, it is a good idea to thread 10 or even 20 needles before you begin. Without cutting, thread them all onto the end of the thread of a single spool. Separate the first needle from the rest by unreeling about 18″ (46 cm) of thread, cut, and knot. Leave the rest of the needles on the spool until you are ready to use them. An added bonus is that all your needles are threaded while your eyes are fresh!

Making the Quilter's Knot

1. Take the threaded needle in the fingers of the dominant hand so that the thread hangs down.
2. With the other hand, draw the tail of the thread up toward the eye of the needle. The tail of the thread meets the tip of the needle head-on.
3. Close the circle by completely, overlapping the needle so that the very end of the tail presses against the eye of the needle.
4. Hold the tail against the needle with one hand.
5. With the other hand, wrap the thread around the point three times in any direction.
6. Push the wraps down toward the eye and hold them down with the index finger and thumb of the dominant hand to keep them from unwinding.
7. With the other hand, grab the point of the needle. Do not let go of the needle and wrapped thread.

Making the Quilter's Knot

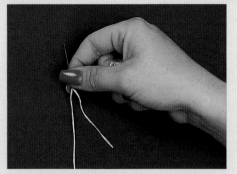

1. Let thread hang down.

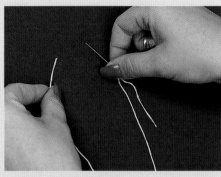

2. Tail meets tip of needle.

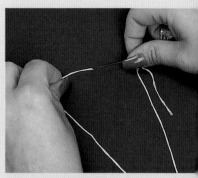

3. Close the circle.

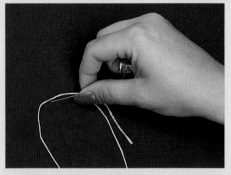

4. Hold tail against needle.

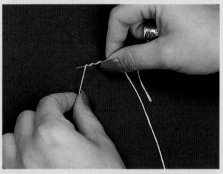

5. Wrap thread three times.

6. Push wraps down and hold.

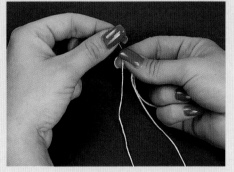

7. Grab point of needle.

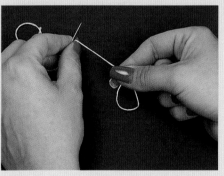

8. Pull threaded needle up and out.

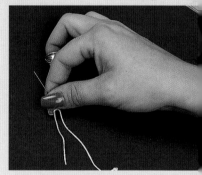

9. A neat knot forms.

8. While still pinching the wraps with the fingers of the dominant hand, pull the threaded needle up and out the full length of the thread.

9. By the time the end of the thread is reached, a neat consistently sized knot will form somewhere between ¼″ to ½″ (0.5 cm to 1 cm) from the end of the thread. Do not trim off the tail of the thread or the knot might manage to untie itself between the layers of the quilt. The size of the knot is important. If it is too small, it might pop out, and if it is too big, it might damage the weave of the fabric in the quilt top.

Beginning to Quilt

Always begin stitching in the middle of the quilt, not at the outer edges. This way, you avoid inadvertently locking ripples in the center. Also, as you work from the center out to the edges, it is much easier to keep all the layers smooth and aligned.

A quilt is never worked from the back, always from the front. To hide the knot, insert the needle about ¾″ (2 cm) from the point you wish to start quilting. Push the needle through the quilt top and the batting, but not through the backing. Skip the needle between the layers and bring the point up to the surface at the precise spot where you decided the quilting should begin. When the knot stops, gently pop it into the center of the quilt. Push the yarns of the fabric where the knot has passed back into position by running a fingernail over the surface of the quilt top.

One of my quilts, *Wedding Rings and Champagne Bubbles on a Bed of Roses* (see page *vi*), came back to me from a national competition with only one criticism from a judge who stated, "When the quilt is held up to the light, the tails of the threads do not go in the right direction." I concluded the only way to keep this criticism from showing up again in the future would be to run the needle between the layers *along a line of quilting or along a line to be quilted*. That way, all the tails are camouflaged along the line! A hidden benefit turned out to be once in a while I actually quilted back over some of those tails and it reinforced my quilting!

Making the Stitch

Fast, efficient, and easy to learn, the quilting stitch, once mastered, results in small even stitches that turn a beautifully designed quilt into a fine piece of handwork. Because it causes virtually no stress on the hand or fingers, a quilter who uses the quilting stitch correctly can work quickly and for longer periods, with the last stitch as perfect as the first.

1. Balance the needle at a perpendicular 90° angle through the layers of the quilt between the middle finger of the top hand and the index finger of the bottom hand. No other part of the hand should touch the needle. Do not push on the needle yet; you will know if you do, because your bottom finger will hurt!

2. Without pushing on the needle, causing it to advance through the fabric, gently lay the needle backward. The finger

underneath pushes up forcefully to ensure that the needle does not advance farther than it should. Move the thumb into position on the quilt near the point at which the needle will resurface.

3. Lay the needle all the way back so that the tip is pointing up. The thumb should be pushing down forcefully on the quilt top immediately in front of the needle tip. (I even dig grooves in the nail polish on my thumb to keep the needle from slipping.) The underneath finger continues to push the needle up so that it will resurface as quickly as possible. Only at this time, when the thumb has pushed *down* and the finger from below is pushing *up* hard, push on the needle and take the stitch. *Stop pushing* as soon as the needle tip is visible.

4. With the needle gently caught in a dimple on the thimble, gently *lift* it back up to a perpendicular angle so that it can barely be felt by the index finger below. This is strictly a rotational movement; the needle should not advance any farther through the fabric.

5. Once the needle is back up to the perpendicular position, you are ready to begin the second stitch. This is exactly the same position as Step 1, except there is now a stitch stacked on the needle.

6. The underneath finger can now stop pushing *up*, allowing the thimble finger to push the needle *down*. The underneath finger should be feeling for the needle tip to clear the fabric. As soon as you feel it, *stop pushing*!

7. Repeat Step 1 to Step 6 to stack a second, third, and fourth stitch on the needle. Pull the needle through the stack of stitches to the end of the thread and then give a gentle tug to tighten. Pull the thread through with the same tension with every stack of stitches to result in a consistent, even line of quilting.

8. The number of stitches you can stack varies with the size of your stitches. The general rule is when you can no longer pivot the needle back up to a full 90° angle, it is time to pull through. The needle may bend with stitches on it and you will definitely appear to warp the fabric, but the needle did rotate all the way up. Probably one more stitch and it will be time to pull through.

1. Correct

2. Incorrect

3. Incorrect

The Quilting Position

1. **Correct quilting position.** *Quilt toward your body whenever you have an option. Keep the shoulder down and relaxed, the elbows down, the wrist straight, and the fingers gently curved and relaxed.*

2. **Incorrect position.** *The raised shoulder causes the back to lean, the elbow tight against the side, the wrist bent backward, and the fingers stiff. This position causes pain and can lead to such conditions as arthritis, carpal tunnel syndrome, tendinitis, and headaches.*

3. **Also incorrect position.** *Keep shoulders and elbows down, but relaxed.*

Making the Stitch

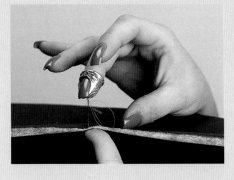

1. *Balance needle at 90° angle.*

2. *Lay needle backward.*

3. *Take stitch.*

4. *Lift needle back up.*

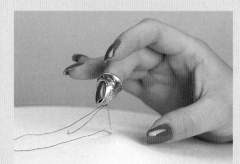

5. Back to 90° angle.

6. Feel for the needle tip.

7. Take second stitch.

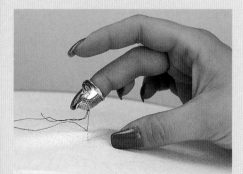

8. When you cannot return needle to 90° angle, pull through.

This sequence of photographs shows the precise positions of the top and bottom hands during the quilting stitch. Done correctly, the stitch causes no stress on the hands or fingers and results in small, even stitches.

Hiding the Knot

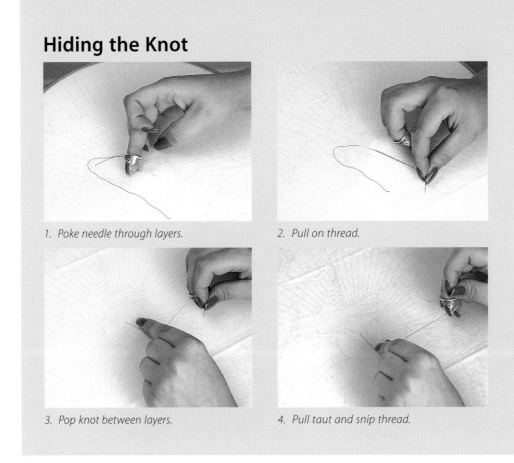

1. *Poke needle through layers.*

2. *Pull on thread.*

3. *Pop knot between layers.*

4. *Pull taut and snip thread.*

How to Stop Quilting

When the thread is down to about 6″ (15 cm) long, it is time to knot-off. Loop the thread round in a circle. Bring the needle up through the circle. Hold the circle down with a finger while reducing its circumference by pulling on the threaded needle. The goal is to get the knot to form about ¼″ (0.5 cm) from the quilt top. Poke the needle back through the same hole from which it exited the quilt, jump at least ½″ (1 cm) between the layers, resurface, and "pop" the knot between the layers. Cut the thread close to the quilt top. After threading a new needle, jump through the layers and bring the needle back up through that same hole you made when you knotted off. This way, from the back of the quilt, it will not look as though you missed a stitch.

Stitches Per Inch

A perfect line of stitching is, most importantly, an even line of stitching. Even quilting is achieved when all the stitches and all the spaces between the stitches on the front and on the back of the quilt

How to Stop Quilting

1. Loop thread around in a circle.

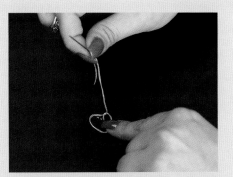

2. Bring needle up through circle.

3. Pull on threaded needle to form knot.

4. Jump needle between layers and pop knot.

are exactly the same length. Just as you hear rhythm in music, you can *feel* rhythm in quilting. With practice, you can feel that the needle is in exactly the right place and can react at exactly the same instant with every stitch. As you rock back and forth, you know the momentum is steady and the stitches are perfectly spaced. As with any other skill, practice makes perfect! Periodically, measure your stitches to keep track of how well you are quilting. Use the simple gauge on page 73 as a guide.

How many stitches are there per inch in a perfect line of quilting? Here is a simple gauge by which you can judge your progress:

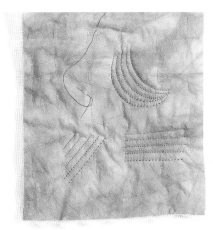

6 stitches per inch = Accomplished	(2.5 stitches per cm = Accomplished)
8 stitches per inch = Average	(3 stitches per cm = Average)
10 stitches per inch = Expert	(4 stitches per cm = Expert)
12 stitches per inch = Professional	(5 stitches per cm = Professional)
14 stitches per inch = Micro Quilter	(5.5 stitches per cm = Micro Quilter)
16 stitches per inch = Weaver!	(6 stitches per cm = Weaver!)

Getting Off on the Wrong Foot

Unfortunately, many beginning quilters start off on the wrong foot by using a basic stitch that they have taught themselves or, worse still, have learned from others. Here are two common styles of hand sewing that will never result in That Perfect Stitch.

Stab Stitching

Stitch by stitch, the left hand "stabs" the needle at a perpendicular angle through the quilting layers, while the right hand waits underneath to grab it and pull it through. Once a little thread is through, the needle is turned around and poked back up through the layers, where the left hand is waiting to grab it and start the process again. After eight or ten stabs, the thread is pulled through. Besides being slow and cumbersome, stab stitching usually results in sloppy, uneven stitches, mainly because, when working from the underside, it is impossible for the quilter to see exactly where the stitches are going. This technique is aggravated still by quilters who use their dominant hand on top instead of below. More control is needed below, where the quilter does not have the advantage of sight.

Running Stitch

It is easy to look at a quilt and conclude that the quilting stitches resemble a simple line of running stitch. Beginner quilters, especially those who are self-taught, use the running stitch, holding the needle between the index finger and thumb and guiding it through the layers. Some use a thimble on the middle finger to help the needle along. While it is easy for novices to learn, the running stitch has its drawbacks. First, it is stressful on the joints of the fingers, because of the "pinching pressure" needed to guide the needle up and down through the layers. Second, it is very difficult to achieve small even stitches, especially when quilting through seam allowances. More than 10 stitches per inch (4 stitches per cm) is impossible, since the needle cannot be turned around in a short enough space to achieve a perpendicular angle on both the down-thrust and the up-thrust.

No matter how tiny you make your stitches, remember that *evenness*, not size, is the single most important element of quilting. Quilt appraisers prefer an even 8 stitches per inch (3 stitches per cm) to a sloppy 12 (5). If a quilter has gained enough control to produce even stitches, then it's much easier to increase the number of stitches per inch (cm). If you concentrate on making your stitches even rather than small, you will very soon develop a rhythm. Interestingly, my experience has been that the larger the stitches, the more difficult it is to make them straight and even. Try Workshop 1 below and you will see what I mean—it is very challenging, but it will teach you a lot about the quilting stitch.

There is another reason why size of stitches is not all-important. The stitches you make must be appropriate to the quilting design you are following. Obviously, the quilt design should match the theme of a quilt, and if bigger stitches are more suitable, so be it. I have even met fine quilters who simply do not like the look of 14 stitches per inch (5.5 stitches per cm). The point is, you must experiment to find That Perfect Stitch for you and for the quilt you are making.

Quilter's Workshop

1. Sandwich 18″ (45 cm) squares of fabric, batting, and backing together. With a chalk marking pencil, draw five parallel lines on the fabric. With a very visible quilting thread, quilt along the first row, deliberately attempting just 6 even stitches per inch (2.5 stitches per cm). When you are finished, go on to the next row and quilt 8 stitches per inch (3 stitches per cm). Finish the next lines with 10, 12, and 14 stitches per inch (4, 5, and 5.5 stitches per cm). Remember that it will not be possible to make 14 stitches per inch (5.5 stitches per cm) unless you selected a fabric with a good thread count (see page 2) as well as a good hand-quilting batt (see page 12).

2. The easiest quilting job is whole cloth—a quilt made of unpieced fabric covered with intricate quilting stitches. Whole cloth is ideal for practicing the quilting stitch. There are no cumbersome seam allowances, and the fabric is the same all over, which means it is easy to develop a rhythm and make all the stitches even. Make a miniature whole-cloth quilt, mark a simple quilting design, and stitch.

CHAPTER TEN

Quilting Techniques

Once you have mastered That Perfect Stitch, you will find that you still have to adjust your technique slightly to handle various situations and directions required by different quilting designs. Even a nice quilting stitch can appear sloppy if made in unnatural directions. As mentioned in the previous chapter, quilting south is the most comfortable and orthopedically correct direction. At a frame you may not be able to turn your quilting line toward you, so adjust the angle you are sitting at to position the line correctly. Some cases require short periods of creative quilting, such as thumb quilting, in order to work away from yourself. In this chapter you will learn about these and other common situations a quilter will encounter.

*Bottom to top: **Tricycles and Trains** (in drawer) by Roxanne McElroy; **Les Sirenes (The Mermaids)** by Roxanne McElroy; **Jewell's Paradise** by Roxanne McElroy; **Victorian Orchid** by Dierdra McElroy; **Scottish Thistle** by Roxanne McElroy; **Mermaids in the Surf** by Roxanne McElroy; **Ia Orana** by Dierdra McElroy; **Wedding Rings and Champagne Bubbles on a Bed of Roses** (hanging down) by Roxanne McElroy.*

With the Grain

Ideally, we would all like always to be able to quilt diagonally across the grain of the fabric. Quilting parallel with the grain causes problems, because quilting thread is naturally inclined to "kiss up to" the nearest yarn of fabric running parallel with it, which makes some of the stitching disappear. This happens more frequently with thread that is not waxed, because the lighter weight matches the weight of the yarns in the fabric itself. Be careful, too with fabrics with a 60/60 thread count, because the yarns of these fabrics are actually heavier than the heaviest quilting thread!

Thumb Quilting

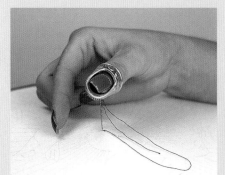

1. Balance needle at 90° angle.

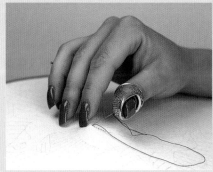

2. Lay needle down.

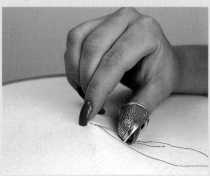

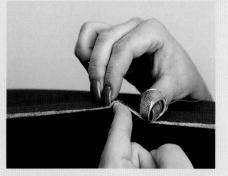

3. Take stitch.

The principle of thumb quilting is exactly the same as the normal quilting stitch, but the thumb and middle finger reverse roles. Work slowly and wear a thimble on your thumb to minimize pressure. The thumb rotates and pushes the needle, while the forefinger pushes the fabric down in front of the needle before it resurfaces.

Quilting in Straight Lines

Quilting *south*—or quilting toward you—is the easiest direction in which to quilt, simply because of the natural location of your thumb in relationship with your hand. It also allows for relaxed shoulders, elbows, and wrists so that you can quilt better for longer periods of time. It is a good idea, when quilting on a hoop, always to quilt south. On a full frame, however, this is not as easy, though a quilter soon learns to twist around on her chair in order to quilt toward her. There are times when you will need to quilt *north*—or away from you—for example, to avoid having to knot-off the thread and re-enter from the opposite direction. *Thumb quilting*, as it is called, takes practice, but means that you can quilt north for short lengths and still achieve That Perfect Stitch. Sometimes when thumb quilting, you may feel your stitches are not quite straight. When you pivot the needle back, make sure that it is lying along the quilting line before you push for the stitch. If you are a prolific quilter and use a full-size quilt frame, it may be wise to invest in a good thimble for your thumb. Otherwise, temporary fixes might be leather thimbles or a thimble that does not quite fit your thumb but that suffices for a few stitches.

Quilting Curves

The difficulty in quilting a tight curve lies in the fact that there is a limit to the number of stitches you are able to stack as you work around the curve. This means it is difficult to set and maintain an even rhythm while you quilt. No matter how tight the curve, never stack less than two stitches before pulling the thread through the quilt. If you quilt one stitch at a time, it is virtually impossible to maintain evenness of stitches and tension.

Quilting Through Seam Allowances

A common mistake when quilting through bulky seam allowances is to resort to stab stitching, which too often results in uneven and unattractive stitching lines. A simple method of backstitch allows you to maintain That Perfect Stitch. As you approach the seam allowance, instead of setting the needle in front of the point at which the thread emerged from layers, set it one stitch-length behind this point, cutting the length of the stitch space in half. Repeat, one stitch at a time, until you are through the seam allowance and can safely continue the

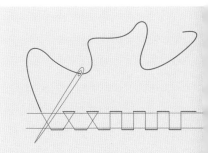

Topsy's Star. Made by Rheba Rozeboom.
The design in the corner squares and the setting triangles are made by using a corner stencil four times. The background quilting accents the feathers. The border feathers look like trapunto because of the amount of background quilting.

Star of the Blue Grass (detail).
Made by Elaine Rothermel, Oxnard, CA.
Trapunto with stippling around the ferns.

speedier quilting stitch. If you have many seam allowances, switch to a needle one size larger so you can exert more pressure.

Jumping Lines

To avoid having to knot-off and re-enter at the end of each line of quilting, jump from one line to the next between the layers. Particularly if you are quilting with dark thread on a light fabric, be sure your needle also goes below the batting to keep the thread from shadowing through the top of the quilt. Jumping lines helps you quilt faster. It also means you have to tie fewer knots, giving you a stronger quilt.

Quilter's Workshop

1. Practice quilting on a curve by tracing four circles of different sizes onto a muslin top. Add batting and backing and put it into a hoop. Start with the largest circle. Quilting curves requires the quilter to take it a little slower. Make sure the tip of the needle resurfaces on the line. I cannot tell you how many stitches to take before pulling through, because it depends on the size of the stitches you are making. The general rule is that when you can no longer bring the needle back up to a 90° angle with all the stitches stacked on it, it is time to pull through. The smaller the circle, the fewer stitches you can take. Try always to do at least two stitches, though, for consistency. Now, move on to the next largest and note the differences between the two.

2. Pull out a quilt that has some seam allowances in it and practice quilting through them. If you do not have a quilt in progress, create a small pieced top by sewing strips together and adding batting and backing. Quilt horizontally across the strips to encounter as many seams as possible. Check the back frequently and compare it to the front. Using a size 9 Betweens will help, as will highly visible thread.

Jumping Lines

Allow room for one last stitch.

Insert needle through top layer and batting only, not backing.

Resurface needle at position you wish to continue quilting.

Pull thread through taut.

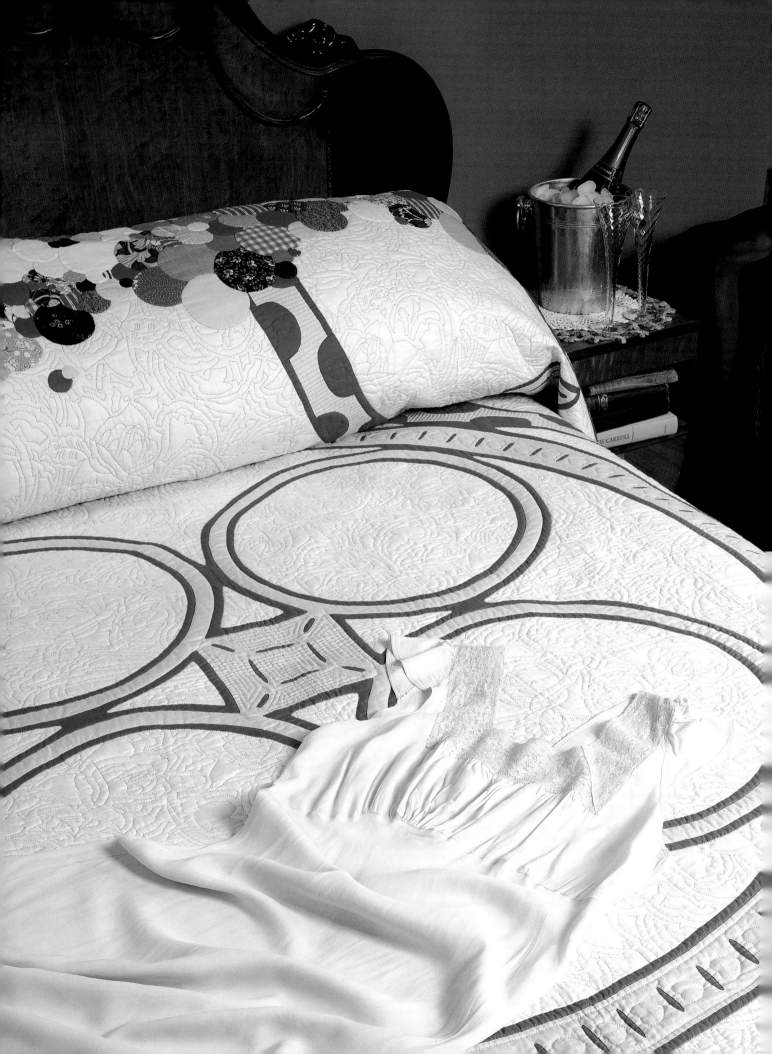

CHAPTER ELEVEN

Quilting Designs

Quilters spend considerable time designing their quilt tops. Once the overall design is chosen, the colors must be exactly right. Sometimes, the quilt top takes as much as a year to finish. Yet it never ceases to amaze me how frequently I hear, "Now I just have to quilt it and it will be done." It is as though the quilting is nothing more than a routine, hurry-and-get-through-it finishing process, one that cannot be ignored but that does not warrant much time. The truth is that even a quilt that has an award-winning design and brilliant color scheme will be reduced to mundane if it has an uninspired quilting design that is poorly executed. Although the quilt design is quilted over the patchwork or appliqué design, it *never* covers it up; it only adds to the quilt's overall look.

Wedding Rings and Champagne Bubbles on a Bed of Roses.
Made by Roxanne McElroy.

Music Music. Made by Elaine Lewis, The Woodlands, TX.
Look at this extraordinary quilting design—the treble clef is stitched all over the quilt.

Choosing a Quilting Design

We are fortunate that today there are many, many different quilt designs to choose from. If you do not create your own design, books and stencils offer all the ideas and help you could want. Remember that even the simplest quilt top requires intricate quilting to make it complete. In fact, I always feel that the simpler the quilt top design, the more intricate the quilting design ought to be. I have never seen an over-quilted quilt! Remember, too, as you choose or create a design that it will take time to finish. An interesting design, though it might seem complicated at first, will hold your attention and keep you from giving up on the quilt out of boredom. The objective, after all, is to end up with a finished quilt you can be proud to call a family heirloom.

I urge you to spend as much time designing your overall quilting design as you spend designing your quilt top. And spend as much or even more time quilting than you spend with piecing or appliqué. I have seen many antique quilts where the fabric has totally rotted away and the entire quilt is held together by the seam allowances and the quilting stitches. The heavier the quilting, the more securely the layers are attached, and the longer your quilt will last. A simple rule of thumb: when in doubt, add more quilting.

A Catalog of Quilting Designs

There are many ways to mark a quilt top. The design and your confidence in yourself have a lot to do with the method you choose. In this chapter, I have provided many of the most common designs, used over the ages, noting how each is best marked onto the quilt top. Each is fairly easy to mark. Remember to consider the overall feel of your quilt before choosing a design. Remember also to test any marking utensil you choose on each fabric in your quilt to be 100 percent sure that the lines can be removed later.

When using templates, I have found that cutting them out of or gluing them to the smooth side of fine sand paper will keep them from slipping while tracing around them. When using stencils, the biggest problem is that the quilter must use a marker with a very fine point in order for it to fit the slots in the stencil. Chalk and graphite pencils seem to work best.

Rare Quilts

To appreciate how special hand quilting is, consider that 50 years from now, there will be 50 times more quilt tops around than there are today. That is because more people are making more quilt tops and not bothering to quilt them. In every other way, these quilt tops will be perfect, because the materials and techniques available to us today ensure that perfection. The supply will be far greater than the demand, and these lovely quilt tops will be worth even less than quilt tops today. It will be hand-pieced and hand-quilted quilts that stand the test of time while unfinished machine-pieced tops languish in closets.

Echo-Quilting

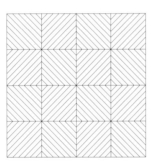

Diagonal Rays

Diagonal Rays, multiple blocks

Echo-Quilting

Traditional Hawaiian quilts are typically echo-quilted. This style is best suited to appliqué quilts. The quilter first quilts close to and around the edges of the appliquéd design. This is called *outline quilting.* That outline is repeated or "echoed," usually every ½″ (1 cm) until the entire surface is quilted. The distance between the lines of quilting does not always need to be ½″ (1 cm); it can vary from ¼″ to 1″ (0.5 cm to 2.5 cm), increasing as the rings move outward. Traditionally, Hawaiian quilters use the width of their thumbs as a guide. *Tiare de Tahiti* on page 10 is echo-quilted.

Another type of echo-quilting is more symmetrical in appearance. This design is meant to look as though a pebble was thrown at the center of a pond, the ripples moving outward. The quilter draws a circle at the center of the quilt, without touching the appliqué, and quilts it. Then, at a predetermined distance, the quilter repeats larger circles until the entire quilt is quilted.

Diagonal Rays

This is an easy and convenient way to fill background areas of a quilt or quilt block. The first line is always drawn diagonally from one corner to the opposite corner with a straight edge. From there, the lines can be drawn as closely as every ¼″ (0.5 cm) or as wide apart as every 1″ (2.5 cm). Often, for convenience, quilters simply use the width of their yardsticks or rulers as a guide. The distance between the lines can drastically affect the overall feel of the quilt, so think carefully about the look you want.

Another option for quilts that have multiple blocks is to change the direction of the diagonal rays in each block. This can sometimes produce a secondary pattern. Sketch it out on paper before committing yourself to the design.

Double Rays

This quilt design is marked in the same way as diagonal rays, except that each line is accentuated by echoing it closely. Try echoing each line at ¼″ (0.5 cm), then separating each set of lines by a full 1″ (2.5 cm).

Crosshatching

Baltimore album quilts are traditionally crosshatched. Crosshatching is achieved by marking diagonal rays in one direction and then repeating them in the other direction. This produces little diamonds across the quilt. The closer the diagonal rays are placed, the more the diamonds seem to puff out in the finished product. *Spring Garden* on page 64 is crosshatched. *Tahitian Hibiscus* on page 54 has a double crosshatch design. The stitches are identical in size on the front and back.

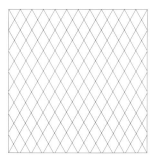
Crosshatching

Double Crosshatching

This design adds more interest. Mark double rays diagonally across the quilt and then repeat diagonally in the other direction. Double crosshatching can give a plaid look, especially when done in different colored threads.

Double Crosshatching

Stitch-in-the-Ditch

Stitch-in-the-ditch is the most laborious type of quilting. The quilter simply quilts as close as possible to all the seams. It is difficult, because seam allowances come into play, requiring the quilter to wrap several layers of fabric over the needle for each stitch. To think that some teachers still recommend this design to beginners! Some quilters quilt ¼″ (0.5 cm) away from each seam to avoid the hardship of seam allowances. This is fairly effective, but you usually end up quilting with the grain, which is not easy either. Still, stitching-in-the-ditch is a good way to accentuate certain areas of piecing or appliqué. *Desert Storm* on page 6 features some stitch-in-the-ditch.

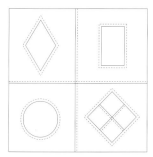
Stitch-in-the-Ditch

Forgetting for a moment the difficulty of stitch-in-the-ditch, consider the overall effect on the quilt. It seems to me that if a quilter has gone to the trouble of piecing together dozens of shapes, painstakingly matching the points and creating a visual line, why waste time duplicating that line? Quilting over your piecing or appliqué never covers your quilt top, it only adds to it. Actually, all the more reason to choose a completely different design to add to your top rather than duplicate it.

Trellis

This design is accomplished by marking diagonal rays from one corner of the quilt to the other, and then marking vertical or horizontal lines across the quilt. In contrast to crosshatching, the diamonds are angled in trellis.

Trellis

Double Trellis

For double trellis, first crosshatch your quilt. Then, add vertical or horizontal lines across the quilt. For a symmetrical look, make sure that each row of diamonds produced by the crosshatching (or every other one) is cut in half by a vertical or horizontal line.

Double Trellis

Stippling

Stippling is a quilting technique in which the quilting lines are placed closely together, creating a flat but softly graded look. The look achieved can be very random or very angular. The most popular form of stippling is produced by creating a meandering line of quilting that never crosses itself but wanders over the quilt, with no less than ⅛″ to ½″ (0.3 cm to 1 cm) between lines. *Shamrock Fantasy* on page 22 uses stippling.

Stippling

Clamshell

This rather complicated design can be marked quite easily and can provide a fascinating effect. First, decide how far apart your quilting lines will be, and then how many layers each shell will have. Tie a string to your marking utensil. If, for example, you decide each line should be ½″ (1 cm) apart and you want each shell to have four layers, then tie four knots in your string, ½″ (1 cm) apart. Begin at one corner of the quilt top and hold the knot that is closest to your pencil down on that corner. With the string taut, place the tip of the pencil at the edge of the quilt and mark the curve until you reach the other edge. Then repeat this motion, but hold the next knot at the corner instead. This will produce a second curve ½″ (1 cm) away from the first. Repeat with the third and fourth knots. To begin the next layer of clamshells, hold the farthest knot from your pencil on the edge of your quilt where the last line you marked touches. This will become your new corner. Mark your four curves and then hold the knots at the other side of the quilt. Once you get past this point, use the intersections between last lines of clamshells as your corner to pivot your string from. You will create a pyramid effect of clamshells. The first line has one clamshell, the next line has two, and so on.

Stippling, Alternate

Stippling, Alternate

Clamshell

Champagne Glass

This design was traditionally marked with champagne glasses and the size of the circles is determined by the size of the glass used. First, find the center of your quilt and mark a straight line across it. Then, either tracing around a glass or using a compass, mark a row of circles along that line. You can either use the center line to match the top of the glass or have the line going down the imaginary center of the circles. Be sure to overlap each circle consistently by a predetermined amount. For the second row, overlap the circles again sideways by the same amount, and make sure the whole row overlaps the bottom row by that amount, too. When you reach the edges of the quilt and there is not enough room for an entire circle, trace the circle anyway, allowing it to run off the edges. *Balloons over New Mexico* on page xxii uses the champagne glass design.

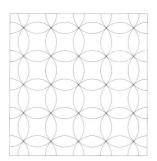

Champagne Glass

Too Much Champagne!

This design can provide an interesting effect to the right quilt by causing the eye to wander randomly over the quilt until the viewer discovers there is not symmetry to the pattern at all. You can do this with any geometric or even non-geometric shape. Simply trace whatever outline you choose randomly onto the quilt top, without regard to symmetry or to the number of shapes per block. Try using lollipops, a teddy bear, flowers, or candy canes. This could quickly approach a stippling design, depending on how closely you quilt.

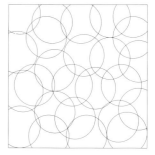

Too Much Champagne!

Outline Quilting

Not to be confused with echo-quilting or stitching-in-the-ditch, when outline quilting, the quilter takes inspiration from the fabric itself for the quilt design. If you have a dominant fabric in your quilt that has an interesting pattern, use that pattern as your template and quilt it. The advantage is that you do not have to mark the design, it is in the fabric already. Outline quilting can be quite striking when color threads are used on a white-on-white quilt. If the fabric you want to outline is not dominant, you can trace the design to create your own template and move it around randomly or in a predetermined pattern across your quilt. *Ia Orana* on page 43 is outline-quilted.

Stippling, Alternate

Stippling, Alternate

Feathers

Certainly one of the most elegant of all the traditional quilting designs, feathers are not nearly as difficult to mark as you might think. First, draw a line in the direction in which you wish the feathers to go. The line can be straight, curved, or a combination. Then, lay a penny against the left-hand edge of the bottom of the line. (Imagine that the

Outline Quilting

Marking Feathers

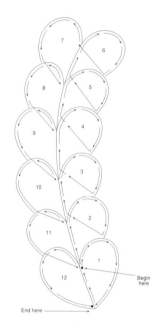

Quilting Feathers

3 o'clock point on the coin is touching the line.) Trace around the penny from the 12 o'clock point to the 6 o'clock point. Slide the penny upward, the 3 o'clock point still touching the directional line and the 6 o'clock point touching the top of the first feather, to stack another feather on top of the one you have drawn. Draw around the penny, line-to-line. Continue up to the top of the directional line, then repeat on the right-hand side of the line. Notice that if your line is curved the feathers on either side of it will not match up in placement.

Feathers can be quite confusing to quilt. They must be quilted in a direction that flows, as if you are drawing them, or the end product will look unnatural or even sloppy. Start at the bottom inside line of the feather. Work up, out, and around the first and second feather until you come to an intersection. Then, insert the needle between the layers and jump over to the third feather above the one you just finished, starting again at the bottom. Quilt down and around the feather to the next intersection. Then jump through the layers diagonally to the next feather. Continue until the pattern is finished. *Circles and Stars* on page 94 is a wonderful example of quilting feathers.

Trapunto

Trapunto is a technique that adds dimension to specific areas of a quilt. Traditionally, a surgery-like procedure was performed on a finished quilt, whereby the back was opened up so that extra stuffing could be inserted, creating hills and valleys in the quilt. Many less invasive ways to achieve the same effect have since been developed. Some quilters use batting, others yarn or stuffing for trapunto. *Star of the Blue Grass* on page 82 and *Shamrock Fantasy* on page 22 are both excellent examples of trapunto.

A Quick Start to Creating Your Own Quilting Designs

It is not difficult to design a unique and interesting background quilting design. It does not take a lot of artistic talent either. One of the easiest ways of starting your own design is to look around for a shape or a subject that interests you or that is related to your quilt. Then simply trace it onto your quilt top. I created the design of *Wedding Rings and Champagne Bubbles on a Bed of Roses* on page vi this way. It is far less complicated than it looks.

First, I traced an image of a rose at random several times on a very large sheet of tracing paper—36″ × 36″ (90 cm × 90 cm). I flipped the paper over several times to give the rose image a slightly different look. I also varied the shapes of the petals each time to add variety. Next, I did the same with a leaf. Notice that they lie close to, but not touching, the traced roses. I took care, too, that they were not in identical positions around the roses, for a more natural look. The most demanding part of this design was to come up with a couple of vine shapes that pleased me. I placed the vines in the largest spaces between the roses. Last, I quilted thorns—since no marriage is without them!

If you decide to create a floral design like this, remember that there really are no rules. You can trace the rose in whatever size you want, you can turn it over and over again to vary the position; you can place the leaves and vines wherever you like them; and you can alter the sizes of any of the images to fit the spaces on your quilt. You can fill in empty spaces with whatever shapes or images you want. Fill an 8½″ × 11″ (210 cm × 280 cm) sheet of paper with your design.

Once the paper is full, start tracing onto the quilt. As you work on different areas of the quilt top, move the paper around to give the quilting design a more natural, random look. If your quilt top is light in color, it is easiest to place the paper behind the top and trace the design with a quality chalk pencil. Then, sandwich the quilt and baste it, or put it into the quilt frame. If your quilt top is dark in color, you may need to create a plastic stencil of your design to mark through.

Design ideas are everywhere. I often find inspiration in children's coloring books. Other places I have looked are field guides on birds, flowers, or animals. I even found a marvelous Victorian-style design in a book on wrought-iron architecture. Remember that all you need is a set of lines to follow, so any object or pattern can be reproduced in a line drawing and then quilted.

When you begin choosing or designing your own quilting design, the key is to explore the possibilities offered by the overall theme and pattern of the quilt. When you first plan your quilt and while you work on fabric selection, piecing, or appliqué, think about the quilting design. Try to find a design that is completely in tune with the feel of the quilt. If your quilt top is made of pretty floral fabrics, you may choose a subtle, elegant design. But it's much more creative to design a boy's quilt with quilted sports equipment and untied shoes with very long shoestrings as filler design than to do a trite crosshatch. The idea

Rose

Leaf

Thorns

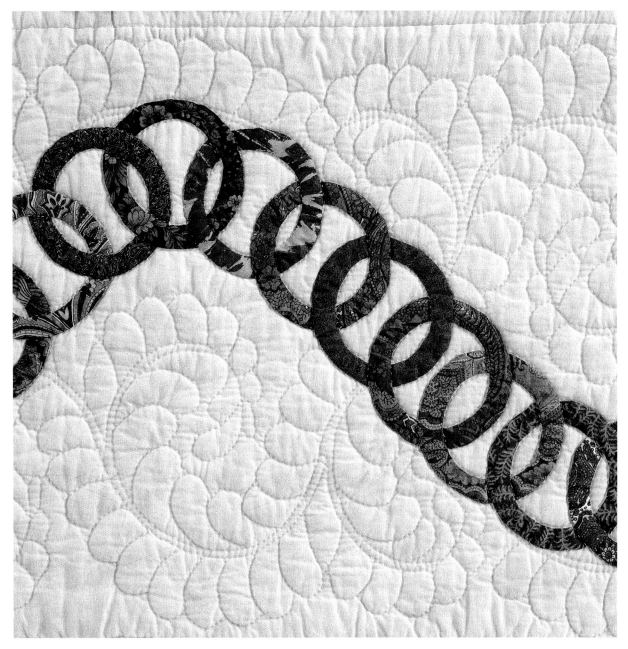

Circles and Stars. Made by Rheba Rozeboom.
*The circles are interlocked by hand appliqué. The feathers in the quilting
design complement the motion of the circles in the quilt top.*

is to experiment. Let your imagination run free, doodle a little, and look for ideas wherever you go. You'll enjoy it—and your quilt will have a design like no other!

Quilter's Workshop

1. On a sheet of 8½″ × 11″ (210 cm × 280 cm) paper, create a quilting design for a baby or holiday quilt. Begin by making a list of items associated with babies, such as bottles, bears, blocks, and bibs. For a holiday quilt, examples might be candy canes, gingerbread men, flags, hearts, or birthday candles. Next, evaluate each object for its overall outline shape. Is it recognizable by outlines alone? Perhaps more than one object would be fun, with a "filler" in between them. Save this paper for future reference—you never know when you may need it!

2. On a sheet of 8½″ × 11″ (210 cm × 280 cm) paper, practice rotating and flipping a design to fill the paper, as if it were the quilt you were marking. Basic shapes such as oddly shaped triangles, hexagons, or uneven parallelograms can be used. Also try more complex shapes, such as flowers, trees, teddy bears, or candy canes. Save everything you finish for future use. The whole sheet of paper can become your pattern, repeating across the quilt.

CHAPTER TWELVE

Taking Care of Handmade Quilts

Aquilter's greatest accomplishment is not to design a wonderful quilt, but to finish it. With hand quilting, where so many hours are invested in making all those perfect stitches, there is no greater joy or reward for the quilter than to finish her quilt. I think the reason that fine antique quilts are so highly prized is that not only do we admire the art of the creator, but we respect the amount of time she dedicated to her work. Since handmade quilts have so much thought, care, money, and time invested in them, it is important that once finished they are treated well. To make a quilt a true heirloom, both the quilter and those who inherit it from her must take the best possible care of it and so expand its life span.

The quilt behind is the backing of **Mermaids in the Surf** *(see page 4).*
The quilt in front is **Scottish Thistle** *(see page 60). Above is a name label from*
Tricycles and Trains *(see page 26).*

Myomi. Made by Elaine Lewis, The Woodlands, TX.

A simple crosshatch makes a perfect background to accentuate this lovely quilt top design.

Hand-Washing Quilts

The way quilts are valued today, there is no reason why a family heir-loom quilt should ever have to be washed, unless, of course, an accident occurs which requires it. Most family heirloom quilts are kept tucked away out of danger or displayed on a guest-room bed. They are rarely used.

It is always best to hand-wash fragile quilts in a very mild soap. Orvis soap, available in quilt shops, was originally developed by veterinarians to be used on the extremely delicate hides of horses. Two tablespoons in 3″ to 4″ (8 cm to 10 cm) of water in a bathtub is a good formula. I always wash my feet and step into the tub with the quilt. Then, using a plunger I purchased specifically for this purpose, I very gently plunge the quilt. Drain the soapy water, refill the tub with clean water, and plunge again to rinse. Drain the rinse water and plunge to extract as much water as possible. Wrap the quilt in clean dry towels and carry it outside. Spread the quilt out on a clean sheet on the grass, cover it with another clean sheet, and allow it to dry. In the winter, smaller quilts and wall hangings can be placed between two towels flat on a floor or large countertop. Keep the washing of larger quilts for spring or summertime, if possible. In an emergency, clean spills by spot washing so that only a part of the quilt gets wet.

Machine-Washing Quilts

Washing machines are amazing these days and my new one has a delicate cycle that is more gentle than I could be washing by hand. Therefore, I do not see that machine washing could do any damage to a new quilt or one that is in very good condition. I would not, however, recommend drying a quilt in the dryer, even on the air setting, since the tumbling action is not kind to quilts. The last 15 minutes of drying in a dryer is the critical point. If you are not sure of the exact temperatures of your dryer's settings, do not chance it.

Ironing Quilts

Many quilters and quilt owners over-iron their quilts. As we saw in Chapter 1, ironing risks damaging the fibers of the fabric. It also tends to flatten any loft created by the batting. You may need to iron after washing, but always use a low setting and press as lightly as you can. Cotton can scorch in seconds if the iron rests too long in one spot.

Quilts and Beds

It should come as no surprise that the best way to store a quilt is to lay it flat on a bed. I have a friend who is a prolific quilter and she frequently invites people into the guest room to view her quilts. It is very pleasant to stand there while she peels back the quilts one by one. Keeping quilts spread on a bed in this way prevents fold lines, which eventually will become stress points, causing the quilt to deteriorate.

Displaying Quilts

Direct sunlight is ruinous to fiber, and quilts should never be placed on a bed or hung on a wall that is in sunlight. If you are considering displaying an heirloom quilt on a bed, observe that bed at various times of day throughout the year to ensure that the sun never directly touches it. Before you decide to display a quilt, consider the climate in which you live, too—humidity causes quilts to deteriorate more quickly.

When hanging a quilt, make sure the quilt has equal support all along the hanging edge. The way to do this is to cut a strip of fabric 8" (20 cm) wide and as long as the quilt is wide. Sew the two edges of the strip together along the long edge to form a tube. Flatten the tube and tack it securely to the top edge of the quilt. Insert a pole through the tube and hang the quilt on the wall. Be sure direct sunlight does not fall onto the quilt. Also, make sure that it is not hanging directly over a heating duct that will cause damaging hot air to pass over the quilt.

There is a wonderful new display system on the market called Displayaway, by Zellerwood Originals. A simple rod system holds the quilt securely in position, while making it easy to insert and remove. The pretty wood panel showcase is a great dust-block! This system is the least stressful means of displaying a quilt that I have seen.

Storing Quilts

All quilts, handmade, antique or not, should be stored very carefully. The ideal way to store a quilt is to spread it on a bed in a guest room that is never used. Folding a quilt onto a quilt display rack is a good idea. Keep it out of direct sunlight and refold periodically in different ways so it does not get permanent creases.

If you decide to store quilts in a closet, be aware that the natural acids in the wood of shelving and drawers can damage the fibers of a quilt over the long term. Line the shelves or drawers with acid-free tissue paper before placing your quilts in storage. They can also be folded and put into a pillowcase or fabric bag with a zipper.

Transporting Quilts

I personally hand-carry my quilts when traveling, even when taking several to a quilt show. If you have to ship a quilt, put it in a pillow case or fabric bag and then place it in a clean garbage bag. You never know what kind of weather your box is going to pass through.

Additionally, padding, like shredded paper, will protect against unexpected punctures. Use a shipper that has a reliable tracking system, so that you know where your quilt is at all times. Require a signature upon receipt so that you know it has arrived safely. By choosing overnight or two-day shipping, you limit the number of times your package is handled. As a final precaution, insure your quilt for those rare occasions when packages are lost.

Labeling Quilts

There are as many good reasons to label your quilts as there are creative ways to label them. Quilt shows often require quilts to be labeled for easy identification. It also makes sense to label in case a quilt is lost or misplaced. Just as importantly, however, you should label your quilts for the sake of posterity. One day, one of your descendants will recognize the beauty of your quilt and wonder at its history.

To label your quilt, simply write your name, the name of the quilt, year completed, and other information you would like to share onto a piece of fabric and sew it onto a corner of the backing (see page 97). Some artists are quite creative with their labels. I have seen labels shaped like flowers, butterflies, and teddy bears. Artists who are accomplished at photo-transfers enjoy creating personalized labels with their own portraits or with pictures that inspired their quilts. Your quilt might be lucky enough to last 200 years or more—label it so that you, as well as your perfect stitches, are remembered.

Quilt Appraisals

Interestingly, one way to increase the value of a quilt is to have it appraised. A certified appraiser will give you an appraisal sheet that should be kept with the quilt. It will register the names of the maker and owner, the inspiration for the design, and a thorough description of the quilt. The nominal fee charge is well worth a good evaluation.

Questions and Answers

Thinking back over my years of teaching the quilting stitch, I have collected a sampling of the most frequently asked questions. The type of person who is drawn to hand quilting seems to have a perfectionist tendency and is always searching to achieve That Perfect Stitch. Never forget that as the artist you have personally placed every single stitch into your quilt and can see minor flaws. Do not berate yourself too strongly for what you may consider unevenness. Enlist the opinions of other quilters or stand back from you quilt to get an overall look. Separate yourself from the individual stitches. If you still see a problem, refer to the questions that follow. Happy quilting!

Q. How can I stop my needle from slipping off the thimble?

A. Make sure that your thimble has dimples that are deep enough to hold the needle. Check this by holding the needle and placing it in a dimple. Then try to move it around. The needle should not budge sideways across the thimble easily, if at all. If you have determined that the dimples are indeed deep enough and the needle still slips out, it is most likely because the thimble is not being rotated slightly to keep the needle at a 90° angle inside the dimple (see page 37). No matter how deep the dimples are, if you do not keep the thimble in contact with the needle, it will slip out of the dimple.

Q. Why are my stitches underneath the quilt much smaller than those on top?

A. This can be caused by one of two things. The most common cause is that the quilter does not rotate the needle back up to a 90° angle after every stitch. The needle must penetrate all three layers of the quilt at a perpendicular angle in order for the stitches on top to match those on the bottom.

Another cause that some quilters encounter is that their fingers are just too sensitive. For these unlucky few, the finger underneath the quilt feels the top of the needle as it penetrates the layers so quickly that they stop pushing and return the tip to the surface a little too early. During the rotation, they drop a thread or two off the needle, causing smaller stitches or missing stitches altogether. To correct the problem, the quilter must feel the needle come through the fabric slightly farther before stopping and returning to the surface. The only solution is to toughen up the finger. Quilters who tolerate the discomfort for short periods at a time will develop a quilter's callus on the finger which will be a natural barrier and solve the problem. You can also try using New Skin before quilting. This will add an extra layer of protection. See Chapter 8 for other helpful aids that will protect the finger.

There are devices made for underneath the quilt. I usually do not recommend them, because a high degree of sensitivity underneath the quilt is necessary for That Perfect Stitch. However, those with extra-sensitive fingers need something. House of Quilting makes a sticky yellow vinyl square that attaches to the finger tip. Aunt Becky's thimble works well, as does the gorgeous porcelain Needle Glider from Jasmine Heirlooms. Medical wraps do not work as successfully, due to their porous nature. It is difficult to judge the distance that the needle has protruded with anything on the finger, so if you do use a finger protector, go slowly so that you can better judge how far the needle has gone.

Q. *My stitches on top of the quilt are huge. Why?*

A. Using the rocking system, this problem almost always occurs because the quilter accidentally pushes on the needle while trying to rotate it back up to a 90° angle. Instead of pushing, the needle should be caught gently in a dimple in the thimble and simply rotated. It should not advance through the fabric at all yet. It takes a quick wrist movement to go from laying flat to standing upright. This takes some practice and will come as the quilter gains control.

Q. *Why are my stitches much larger on the back of the quilt than on the top?*

A. You are allowing your needle to slip through the layers of the quilt as you rotate the needle down. Strive to achieve a very definite rotate *or* push. Do not do both at the same time. As you rotate, the needle should be gently caught in a dimple and you should be able to manipulate the angle. Your underneath finger should be pushing up exactly below the needle's point. Make sure you are not inadvertently pushing the needle. The bottom finger will know if you are pushing by sending a pain signal to your brain! With a good thimble, you should not need to use your thumb to hold it in place. A finger *and* a thumb on the thimble makes it hard to control, whether you are pushing or just rotating.

Q. *Why is my first stitch in each series always larger than the rest?*

A. Unfortunately, this is the case for most of us. If I have not quilted in a few days, I experience the same problem. Therefore, I never knot my thread until I have warmed up for a few minutes. For beginners, this will continue to be a problem for a few hours of total quilting time. It is purely a matter of balance and control, since there is nothing holding the needle yet. To achieve control, stick the needle into the quilt by half its length at the point at which you want to begin stitching. Place the index finger of the underneath hand on the tip of the needle that is protruding below. Place the thimble on the eye of the needle. Obviously, at this point, if either finger pushes on the needle, the other finger will suffer. Gently hold the needle between the two fingers and move them in tandem upward until the bottom finger can tell that the needle is barely penetrating the fabric layers. There should be pressure on the quilt surface, causing a "mountain" of fabric. The tightening of the fabric fibers around the needle will help hold it in place. Begin pivoting down and back, going into your first stitch. Pivot, do not push down on the needle, or you will chew up the skin of the bottom finger, as well as cause your bottom stitches to be larger than the top ones.

Q. *Why does my needle keep popping out of the fabric as I begin to pivot?*

A. This only happens on the first of a series of stitches, and it is because nothing is holding the needle down yet. Instead of putting the needle in at the recommended 90° angle, try inserting it into the quilt angled slightly toward you. This should stop the popping. Also, try not to put so much pressure on the needle with your thimble at this point. As you learn to control the needle, this problem should disappear.

Q. *Though I feel in control of my stitches, they are still uneven. Why?*

A. One cause could be that when you use your thumb in front of the needle point, as it resurfaces from below, you are facing the pad of the thumb to the point. You should not use the thumb pad to feel for the needle to resurface. Your vision is more acute than your sense of touch, and using the thumb in this manner blocks your vision. With time, as the needle keeps touching the thumb pad, even if it touches softly and without pain, the skin builds up a callus. The callus makes your thumb less sensitive, causing your stitches to be larger and more uneven as you wait to feel the needle come through. Rotate your wrist slightly in toward your body and make sure you are quilting south, toward yourself. This will position your thumb in a manner that will allow you to flatten it in front of the needle tip. The needle should then resurface above your thumb. Keep in mind that if you use the pad of the thumb and slip while pushing the needle, you could hurt yourself.

Another cause of unevenness is that the quilting lines are not quite straight. Each stitch seems to march to the beat of a different drummer. When quilting along straight lines, a good way to avoid this problem is to make sure that when you pivot the needle down and back, it lays along the quilting line and not slightly off to one side. Then, push on the needle to penetrate the layers and make the stitch. When quilting curves, make sure the tip is definitely resurfacing on the quilting line. It is critical to have good lighting when quilting. The extreme tip of the needle is so sharp and fine, it is nearly impossible to see. A good strong light shining over the shoulder opposite your top hand should help you avoid shadows cast by the hand. It will make the very tip of the needle glint, helping you to spot it more quickly, thereby better controlling the stitch.

Q. *Why do I get shoulder and hand cramps, even when I quilt for very short periods of time?*

A. First, consult a doctor if you consistently feel pain. Once your doctor has cleared you of any serious medical conditions, take a careful study of your posture as you quilt. Where do you sit? How do you sit? What technique do you use? A quilter in good health should be able to quilt all day, with the eyes tiring first. Avoid sitting stark upright. Instead, relax in a chair with back support, placing a pillow in the small of your back for added support. I like to quilt with a knee up to support my hoop, so I have a footstool. Place your quilt hoop in your lap. Before you begin quilting, take time to relax. Release all tension, let your shoulders fall, and let your arms rest at your sides. Take a deep breath. Your shoulders should be down, elbows resting against your sides, and wrists only slightly bent toward your body. The fingers and thumb should also be toward your lap, forming a backward letter *C*. This is the correct quilting position. The only adjustments to be made are to lift your arm and bend the elbow more in order to position your hand over your hoop. The shoulders remain down, wrists relaxed. Remember always to quilt south or toward yourself, if you can. This is the most natural and relaxed direction possible. This is especially important for people with arthritis. Any other direction will only aggravate the condition with time.

Q. *Why do my needles constantly bend and break as I quilt?*

A. A certain amount of bending is to be expected. A lot of stress is placed on our needles while creating That Perfect Stitch. Needles should not snap before they bend, so, first, make sure you are using a quality needle (see Chapter 3). If your needle bends every few stitches, you should re-evaluate the conditions under which you are quilting. What fabrics and battings are you working with? If they pose several compromises as discussed in Chapters 1 and 2, you should use a needle that is stronger to handle the pressure. Accept that it may not be possible to obtain as tiny a stitch as you are used to on this particular project. Focus on evenness, instead. I often have to drop to a size 9 Betweens to get through seam allowances or painted fabric. Be realistic about the size of needle you are using—use the one that it takes to get the job done well, not the smallest one possible.

Q. *Is quilting like riding a bicycle, you never forget how?*

A. Well, sort of. Once you get the hang of it, you will most likely always remember the principles behind the technique. However, like riding a bike, if you have not done it in a while, it takes a little practice to get back into the swing of things. I tell my students that learning to quilt is like learning to play the piano—you must practice daily for at least 15 minutes. I even offer to write them notes to take home so that their families will leave them alone!

Q. *Why does my thread constantly knot up on me?*

A. First, make sure that you are using a heavily waxed thread, such as Gutermann or YLI. This will help to a certain degree. The main reason for knotting, however, is that the quilter unknowingly rolls the needle between the thumb and finger toward her body as she pulls the thread through the quilt. After a few times, the thread twists and tangles, and eventually forms knots. To counteract this, I trained myself consciously to roll the needle one turn away from my body every time I pulled the thread through after a series of stitches. This stopped the problem completely.

Q. *Should I be concerned about copyrights on quilting designs I use?*

A. Make sure that the designs you use are not copyright protected. The symbol ©, followed by a name, indicates copyright. Copyright laws are intended to prevent anyone from using an intellectual property, such as a quilting design, for profit. There is a fine line between using a copyrighted design for inspiration and plagiarizing that design. When in doubt, do not use a design without permission. Remember, it is illegal to photocopy a page or pattern from a book that is protected by copyright, even if you are just sending it to a friend because she does not want to buy the whole book. If you wish to enter competitions, be published, or produce patterns, you must obtain written permission from the copyright holder first. If you are making a quilt purely for your own enjoyment and use, there is no need to worry about copyright.

Your own original designs can be copyrighted to prevent others from using them for profit, and I recommend to copyright your designs, even if you do not think of them as works of art. Copyright laws are complicated, so enlist the services of an intellectual property attorney to help you.

Q. *How do I know when I am ready to enter a quilt show?*

A. When you have finished a quilt! I encourage all quilters to enter shows. It can be so thrilling if you go into it with the right attitude. True quilt art is creating what you feel, what turns you on, what makes you happy. Displaying your quilt in a show is the culmination of all the work, a wonderful way to celebrate a major accomplishment. In addition, you get to see the judges' opinions of your quilt, and can listen while show-goers view it, without them knowing you are there! If you have an open mind and take it with a grain of salt, this is the best free advice you could ever get on your quilting. Never enter a show with high hopes of winning. Judging is extremely personal and there are no set guidelines for an award-winning quilt. Do not ever let a judge's comments discourage you from creating a new quilt or completing an existing one.

Lesson Plan

That Perfect Stitch is a nationally renowned quilting class that I have been teaching for several years. Students learn the quantifiable reasons why products work for or against us while we quilt and how to evaluate these products on their own in the future. Breaking down the technique into very distinct steps ensures that each and every student will succeed to the best of his or her ability. I always have at least two students leave the class quilting as nicely as I do, and they only get 45 minutes to one hour of actual quilting time in a three-hour class. Be patient. Describe the process in as many different ways as possible. Some students learn best by reading, others by seeing, and still others by hearing. Cover all three approaches in your class.

Supply Kit

Pre-marked muslin top

Matching muslin backing

Batting

Two quilting needles

Spool of thread in visible colors

Small pair of scissors

Thimble

14″ (35 cm) quilting hoop

I recommend supplying each student with the supply kit before class begins.

Skill Level: Beginner to intermediate

Duration: Six hours, broken up into two three-hour sessions or three two-hours sessions

Size: As space allows. Each student needs a chair and enough table space to lay out the project flat for basting.

First Hour

Chapters 1 and 2 of *That Perfect Stitch*

Explain that fabric is woven to the warp and to the weft, and introduce the concept of stitches per inch (cm). Show samples of different types of fabric—muslin, batiks, hand-dyed, painted, etc., paying special attention to the weave of each. Explain the effect on the stitch of quilting with each fabric type, showing samples prepared before class, if you can. Review prewashing of fabric. Discuss battings, reviewing fiber types, loft, bearding, and the effect of batting type on the quilting stitch. Show quilts made from various batting types, or show samples you prepared before class.

Second Hour

Chapters 3, 4, and 5 of *That Perfect Stitch*

Explain the knap of thread and show samples of different brands. Explain how needles are made, so that students understand the importance of using high-quality needles to achieve That Perfect Stitch. Pass a magnifying lens around the class so that students can see the difference between good and bad needles. Emphasize that the smallest needle is not always the best one to use. Have students try on a variety of thimbles to find the size and brand that is right for them. Discuss each thimble's purpose, unique features, and disadvantages. Explain that quilting causes an enormous amount of stress on the finger, demonstrating how the thimble is used.

Third Hour

Chapters 6, 7, and 8 of *That Perfect Stitch*

Review frames and hoops, referring students to the Resources at the back of the book for information on specific brands. Have students baste their projects as you walk around the room. Demonstrate how to place the quilt in a hoop, showing how to adjust on the warp and weft, never pulling on the bias. Show samples of different markers on sample "quilt sandwiches." Prepare in advance samples that have been washed and ironed to show the damage to fibers. Review the helpful aids in Chapter 8. Mention quilting designs and the importance of choosing a design that complements the quilt top.

Fourth to Sixth Hours

Chapter 9 of *That Perfect Stitch*

Demonstrate the quilter's knot, emphasizing that when done correctly, the knot is resistant to coming undone inside the quilt. In small groups, demonstrate how to begin the first stitch, while the rest of the class listens. Make your explanation as clear as possible, changing the way you express it so that everyone understands.

Again in small groups, demonstrate the quilting stitch. Give ideas on how to balance the needle on that first stitch. Then, slowly manipulate your needle, describing what you are doing. Tell students when to push and when not to push. Explain the importance of rotation and the role of the thumb. Avoid using the words *left hand* and *right hand*; instead talk about the *upper hand* and *underneath hand*. Have students try out the stitch, waiting a few minutes to give them time to get started before you watch them. Correct only one thing at a time, giving them a chance to understand and work on the correction before offering any further help. As students come near the end of their thread, demonstrate how to knot-off.

Be patient and completely confident that they *will* all succeed! Some students take longer than others, some have physical problems that impede their immediate progress (help them find a way around them), and still others have mental blocks from past learning experiences. It is your job to break through all barriers one at a time and give each student confidence.*

During the last half-hour, share the chart showing stitches per inch (cm). Measure each student's work, showing how each has improved over the session.

Finally, discuss how quilts are valued. Encourage students to continue practicing. Mention any quilt shows coming up in the area and encourage them to attend. Above all, remind them that if they are having any difficulties working on a particular quilt to take a good look at the elements in that quilt before they assume it's their own fault. Usually, the tools they are using are to blame!

---

* You will hear "I can't" or "my fingers won't" often. It is more talk than mental attitude. Students really want to quilt well or they would not be sitting in your class. Let them say it, but do not give up on them or get frustrated. They *can* do it!

Resources

The following names and addresses are provided because it is often useful to contact manufacturers directly when you experience problems with or have questions about a quilting product. Many, if not all, of these companies have Research & Development departments that can address your concerns. The manufacturer can also direct you to local stores that carry their products. Alternatively, ask your quilt shop to order items for you. They are usually very receptive to new products and try to meet their customers' needs. Several manufacturers and publishers also have Web pages, where you can discover interesting information on new products and services for quilters.

Quilting Tools and Materials

FABRIC

Alexander Henry Fabrics
2501 South Grand Avenue
Los Angeles, CA 90007

Bali Fabrications
1190 East Napa Street
Sonoma, CA 95476

Concord House
1359 Broadway
New York, NY 10018

Hoffman Fabrics
25792 Obrero Drive
Mission Viejo, CA 92691

Kona Bay Fabrics
3043 Lopeka Place
Honolulu, HI 96817

Lunn Fabrics, Inc.
357 North Santa Fe Drive
Denver, CO 80223

P & B Textiles
1580 Gilbreth Road
Burlingame, CA 94010

Peter Pan Fabrics
1071 6th Avenue
New York, NY 10018

RJR Fashion Fabrics
13748 South Gramercy Place
Gardena, CA 90249

Robert Kaufman Fabrics
129 West 132nd Street
Los Angeles, CA 90061

South Sea Import Fabrics
550 West Artesia Boulevard
Compton, CA 90220

V.I.P. Fabrics
1412 Broadway
New York, NY 10018

BATTING

Fairfield Processing Corp.
PO Box 962
Cardiff, CA 92007

Hobb's Bonded Fibers
PO Box 2521
Waco, TX 76702

Mountain Mist/The Stearns Technical Textiles
100 Williams Street
Cincinnati, OH 45215

Mulberry Silk & Things
210 North Central Street
Rocheport, MO 65279

Quilter's Cotton Batting
3205 Foxgrove Lane
Chesapeake, VA 23321

Warm Products, Inc.
16110 Woodinville-Redmond Road #4
Woodinville, WA 98072

NEEDLES

Clover Needlecraft
1007 East Monguex Street #L
Carson, CA 90746

Colonial Needle Co.
1150 Yonkers Avenue
Yonkers, NY 10704

Wright
85 South Street
West Warren, MA 01092
(Boye Needles)

THREAD

Coats & Clark, Inc.
30 Patewood Drive, #351
Greenville, SC 29615

DMC Thread
10 Port Kearny
South Kearny, NJ 07032

Gutermann
999 Stewart Avenue
Garden City, NY 11530

Sulky of America
3113 Broadpoint Drive
Harbor Heights, FL 33983

YLI Thread
482 North Freedom Boulevard
Provo, UT 84601

THIMBLES

Comfort Thimble
PO Box 442
Gresham, OR 97030

House of Quilting
2530 Adkins Hill Drive
Fayetteville, NC 28306

Roxanne International
3009 Peachwillow Lane
Walnut Creek, CA 94598

FRAMES AND HOOPS

Edmunds Frames
6111 South Sayre
Chicago, IL 60638

Elliott Morgan No-Slip Hoop
2255 North East Porter Road
Blue Springs, MO 64014

Flynn Quilt Frame Co.
1000 Shiloh Overpass Road
Billings, MT 59106

Grace Frame Co.
PO Box 27823
Salt Lake City, UT 84127

Jasmine Heirlooms
50 Fairview Drive
Greenville, SC 29609

Pleasant Mountain Frames
PO Box 2294
Mount Pleasant, TX 75456

QUILTING DESIGNS

The Stencil Company
28 Castelwood Drive
Cheektowaga, NY 14227

Stensource International
18971 Hass Avenue
Sonora, CA 95370

SCISSORS

Fiskars Scissors
7811 West Stewart Avenue
Wausau, WI 54401

Gingher Scissors
PO Box 8865
Greensboro, NC 27419

Other Useful Resources

HAND-DYE SUPPLIES

Pro Chemical & Dye, Inc.
PO Box 14
Somerset, MA 02726

QUILT APPRAISER

Sharon Newman
4525 50th Street
Lubbock, TX 79414

QUILT DISPLAY SYSTEMS

Jasmine Heirlooms
50 Fairview Drive
Greenville, SC 29609

Zellerwood Originals
PO Box 54289
Cincinnati, OH 45254

QUILT MAGAZINES

American Patchwork & Quilting Magazine
1921 Grand Avenue
Des Moines, IA 50309

Chitra Publications
2 Public Avenue
Montrose, PA 18801
(*Traditional Quiltworks, Quilting Today, Miniature Quilts*)

Leman Publications
741 Corporate Circle, Suite A
PO Box 4101
Golden, CO 80402
(*Quilter's Newsletter Magazine, Quiltmaker Magazine, Quilts & Other Comforts*)

Lady's Circle Patchwork Magazine
PO Box 267
Sussex, WI 53089

QUILT PUBLISHERS

C & T Publishing
1851 Challenge Drive
Concord, CA 94520

That Patchwork Place
PO Box 118
Bothell, WA 98041

The Quilt Digest Press
4255 West Touhy Avenue
Lincolnwood, IL 60646

QUILTING ORGANIZATIONS

American Quilter's Society
PO Box 3290
Paducah, KY 42003

International Quilt Association
7660 Woodway, Suite 550
Houston, TX 77063

National Quilt Association
PO Box 393, Suite 550
Ellicott City, MD 21041

QUILT SHOWS

American Quilter's Society
PO Box 3290
Paducah, KY 42003

Mancuso Show Management
PO Box 667
New Hope, PA 18938
(Pennsylvania National Quilt Extravaganza, Pacific International Quilt Festival, MidAtlantic Quilt Festival, World Quilt & Textile Show)

National Quilt Association
PO Box 393, Suite 550
Ellicott City, MD 21041

Quilts, Inc.
7660 Woodway, Suite 550
Houston, TX 77063
(International Quilt Market, International Quilt Festival, European Quilt Market, Quilt Expo)

Quilting Designs

Wedding Rings and Champagne Bubbles on a Bed of Roses

Miscellaneous motifs

Carousel

Hummingbirds

Heart and Rose

Tahitian Hibiscus

Philodendron

Autumn Leaves 1

Autumn Leaves 2

Autumn Leaves 3

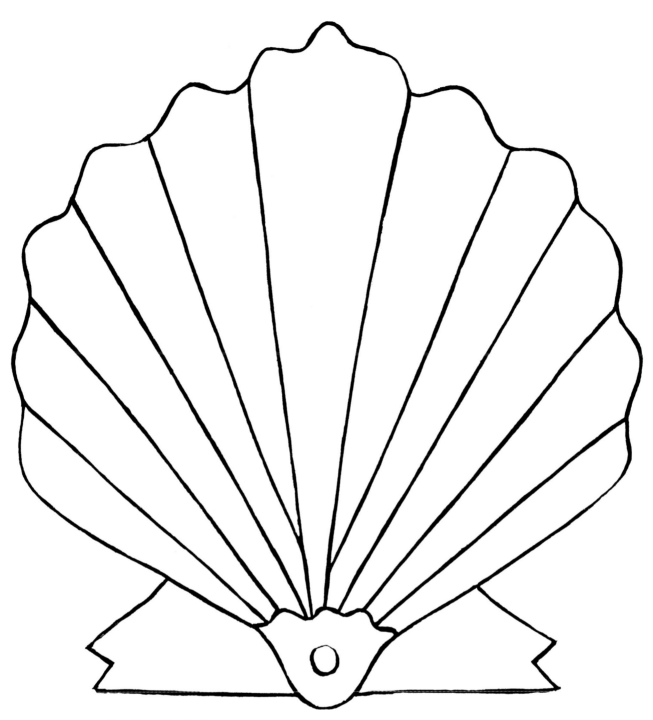

La Coquillage (The Shell)

The Candle

Egg Basket

Heart

Teddy Bear

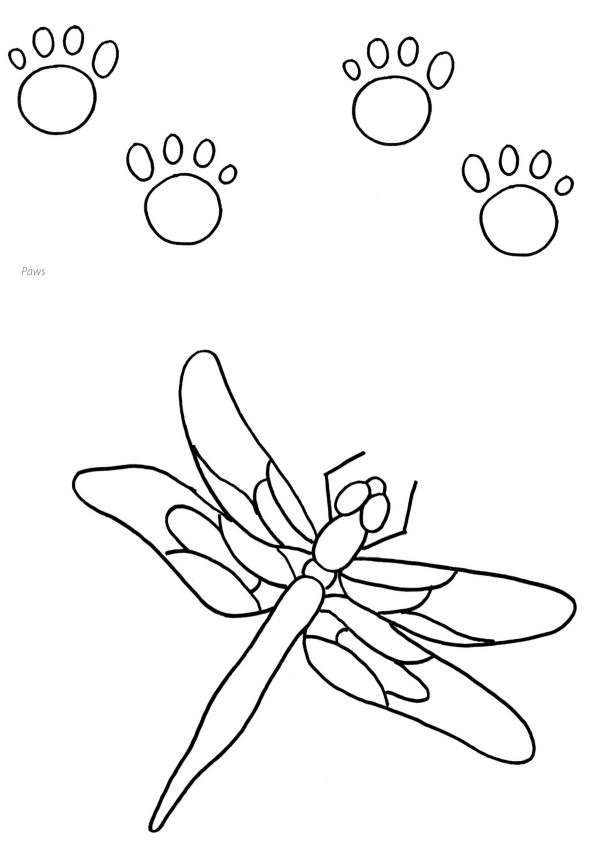

Paws

Dragonfly

Grapes

Star

Gingerbread Man

Bunny

Shamrock

Bird of Paradise

Flowers